Transforming Childhood

A Handbook for Personal Growth

Strephon Kaplan-Williams is an internationally recognised author in the field of growth psychology. He founded the first dreamwork centre, the Jungian-Senoi Institute in America, and works as a therapist as well as lecturing widely on this and related subjects.

By the same author

Changing Your Life
The Elements of Dreamwork
Jungian-Senoi Dreamwork Manual
Seed Bursts
Sources
Transformations 1

Transforming Childhood

A Handbook for Personal Growth

Strephon Kaplan-Williams

Element Books

First published in 1983 by Journey Press

This edition first published in Great Britain in 1990 by
Element Books Limited
Longmead, Shaftesbury, Dorset

Illustrations by Pam Jenkins

Designed by Nancy Lawrence

Typeset in 11/12½pt Sabon Roman by Burns & Smith Ltd., Derby

Printed and bound by Richard Clay Ltd, Bungay, Suffolk

Cover design by Max Fairbrother

Flower illustration by Nemo

British Library Cataloguing in Publication Data
Kaplan-Williams, Strephon
    Transforming childhood: a handbook for personal growth.
    1. Children. Development
    I. Title
    155.4

ISBN 1-85230-152-X

Contents

Foreword

This book contains the gift of life; the rich feeling of life so essential to our well-being and so easily lost to us as we begin to armour ourselves against the awful vulnerability we all experience as children.

Strephon writes with a deep understanding, sensitivity and compassion which is an unusual blend of professional skills and Wounded Child. He brings much of his own feeling nature into the work, enabling the reader to do the same. And there lies the true value, for you will find it difficult to be with this book and remain passive. It calls for response, commitment, involvement, with a compelling and vibrant voice which is difficult to resist.

It is a powerful tool for self-transformation which has worked well for me, many clients, trainees and friends. If you are ready to risk finding more of yourself, to be open to how it really was for you as a child, to begin to redeem the Wounded as well as the Wondrous Child within, then synchronicity has brought a reliable and loving companion to your journey.

The guide has clearly travelled the road himself and shares freely what he has encountered there. You are about to enter a fruitful and challenging relationship – with this book, with Strephon, and of course, with yourself.

Relationship with Strephon is never easy, even through a book. He will make you think and think again. He'll bring you up short, nudging you into reliving old feelings, memories, and once you've fully experienced them, he'll open the way to resolution and healing. He'll infuriate and amuse you. You certainly won't be bored. And he's subtle too, weaving a delicate path through the complexities of life as a child into the potential for life as a conscious, participating adult.

But don't focus too much on the eventual destination. Savour the journey, it has much to offer. Travel well.

For myself, I have travelled much of the way alone. I came into the work through self-taught dreamwork, first of all for my own development and later running dream groups in the South West of England. I feel myself to be a true product of the process, which in many ways I see as an alternative to traditional therapy.

Having trained in Transpersonal Psychology, I began to practise as a Counsellor and Dream Therapist. When I discovered Strephon's books there was a sense of glad recognition and they have certainly made a valuable contribution to my work.

When I was about three years old, my mother flew into a rage and tried to strangle me, a trauma I managed 'to forget' until I was in my thirties. At first I worked on my own with the powerful feelings which came with the memory. Then *Transforming Childhood* helped me to go deeper into my woundedness, and working in training with Strephon proved transformational, enabling me to begin to integrate and heal that terrible experience. This was balanced by some joyous work with my Wondrous Child liberated during my Transpersonal Psychology work. I catch myself sometimes taking a real delight in simple things and expressing it directly through the child.

I joined Strephon as an associate in the summer of 1989 and now run courses in Mandala Dreamwork Training which draw heavily on the books and allow us to combine our ideas and feel for the work.

Collaborating with Strephon and running these courses has proved to be a challenging and invigorating process of its own. My commitment to the work and to my journey is central to my life. I am learning all the time, and the journey goes on.

Maggie Peters, Director
Journey Centre, England

Preface

Anything can happen in reading this material, and will. Think of your experience as one of being born again, only this time you have a second chance to reassess the way in which you handle childhood. It was probably not too good the first time. Somehow, somewhere, the traumas began and we closed off, we tried to leave childhood. We went into fantasy or depression or appeared nice while underneath, deep down inside we hid ourselves from the big people.

Time to come out now! Welcome your long lost child, the child who never got to express herself or himself fully. Take the magical and moving emotional adventure by going through these pages and letting them evoke you. Yes, there are exercises to do, there are always exercises, for how else do we make solid a new learning?

Join with others, and especially those who have worked with this material in our special workshops. Much can be done on your own, but when you add group sharing to the experience then you are supported and moved at even deeper levels.

I would like to think that everyone has a chance to redeem childhood if they would only commit themselves to it. No, we are never over childhood. We can grow up, but without finding and honouring the lost and wondrous child we will always remain hidden to ourselves and others.

With the new edition of this revised and updated work we welcome a whole new audience. May this book fall into good hands, healing hands, ones own and other people's. And may the truth and depth of feeling the words and the work evoke, move its mysteries by word of mouth to those who are searching and would respond to it most.

With love born of the compassion of finding my own lost and wondrous child I welcome this book's readers. It must once again stand on its own in the hearts and minds of others. It will be of good service.

Strephon Kaplan-Williams
Bristol, England

March, 1990

1 The Myth of Childhood

Image: *Once upon a time.*

'Our goal is truly to graduate from childhood.'

We all have a story in us called The Myth of Childhood, which is to say that we are formed at least in part by patterns developed in childhood, and which still rule us in adult life.

A few years ago I threw over the chess board when I made a stupid move in the game and my wife check-mated me. I was having an attack of the Wounded Child archetype. My wounded boy from the past was expressing his feelings. I felt cornered by a superior force and my inability to deal with it. This happens so often in our lives. There we are in some so-called 'adult' situation and our inner child pops up. This is caused by conditioning from the past.

Parents abuse their children and their children grow up in turn to be hard on their own children. The family neurosis can be a terrible legacy to pass down from generation to generation. We fear it. Many will only go back to childhood because they are driven there by a desperate attempt to work out their problems. We return to childhood to face the original trauma and transform it.

On the other hand, your inner child may show up at just the right moments. You are feeling frustrated with a friend or lover and you just laugh and mimic the absurdity of the situation. You have a paper or a letter to write and a new way of saying just the right thing flashes into your mind, recalling that spontaneity you most certainly had as a very young child. Or you are out on a first date and several things you do are a little wild, a little off, and you wonder where that is coming from. You just wanted to have fun that night, didn't you? So did your inner child, perhaps reacting to a rather stuffy or serious person you were making contact with for the first time.

And what if you want to have children but are afraid to because your own childhood was so rough? Your own wounded child archetype lurks just around the corner for you to run into in the darkness of your heart. Until you face your long lost childhood you will have a hard time wanting kids of your own.

We also return to childhood to find the joy which comes with fulfilment based on healing. No matter what the trauma, there is the

1

possibility for healing if we can somehow commit fully to the process of inner transformation as well as outer change. For this, we need guides and sign-posts along the way. This book is full of guide lines for exploration. A lot can be done by responding to the information in these pages. Reading helps, but doing the work is what changes reality.

The Child and Parental Archetypes

There are woes enough in this existence, but before they turn you off to the valuable work, consider this.

The source of creativity is the Wondrous Child, as the source of healing is the Wounded Child. Our full creativity and destiny can only come out when we are deeply in touch with our Child and Parental archetypes. There are wonders to behold still in this adult world, we can return to childhood, not just to suffer, but to find renewal there. In our intimate behaviour we can play, we can be instinctual, creative, as well as dealing with our garbage.

All longing for paradise is a longing to return to the lost childhood we never had. Do not project your longing for a perfect childhood with perfect parents into the sky, into an after-death experience of paradise. Live the transformed life now by integrating paradise within your own soul.

And why talk of other lifetimes as the reincarnationists do? You have only this lifetime to live now. Return to childhood for transformation and you may just redeem your life. No need to return if you have completed your life here. There is no enlightenment until you are reborn into this life.

Childhood

We were born into this life, into a certain environment with a certain set of parents. But living deeply within our psyches already were The Father, The Mother and the Child. We started whole. We had personality dynamics called archetypes. Unfortunately what happened to most of us was that the archetypes within us became only partially fulfilled. If the father is absent our 'inner father' will not develop fully. If the mother plays the father role our 'inner mother' will be broken. If the Child Archetype we are living out as a child gets attacked by the parents, as it often does, then the archetype may undergo a split into the Wounded and the Wondrous Child. The

2

parents play the power game with us, trying to dominate our own development. They cause us to identify with the Wounded Child. We will still experience the Wondrous Child, but we may have to go into fantasy to do it.

In other words, from a harsh childhood we learn to withdraw.

Even if we had an easy childhood we may still feel lost or not understood. The natural parents will only be able to constellate certain aspects of the parental and child archetypes. We carry deep wounds into adult life.

The greatest wound of all is not having the archetypes fulfilled in the actual experience of life. Thus we enter the adult world physically ready, but hardly able to function psychologically as adults. We enter adult life and marry our parents. The archetypes seek fulfilment, we mate with our peers, and in the new bond seek that which we did not realise in our first childhood.

Adult relationships are themselves the second childhood. Not many grow up in their own life-times. They may have jobs, raise children, become old together, but the symptoms are there in childish and dependent ways.

Consider all the compulsions, alcoholism, the dependency syndromes, the governments run by power-hungry, booze-drinking men and women? The disease is not even alcoholism, for beyond that, the compulsives suffer from an unresolved childhood. No one is self-destructive or destructive of others who has resolved their own childhood.

Need we mention all the split relationships and all the relationships which have lasted too long? If we have not solved the dependency problem we have not become adults. If we have not solved the dependency problem, we are, like most of us, adult children caught irretrievably in the Myth of Childhood, the pattern that keeps us immature.

Our long-term goal is to leave childhood by integrating the Child and Parental archetypes inside us, rather than projecting them outwards onto parents, lovers, authority figures, God and Government.

The Process

Our process is a simple one based on direct experience. Using the chapters in this book you will cover major archetypal experiences of childhood. By re-experiencing any of them now, working with the material and the questions, and doing the exercises suggested, you will enter into a deep transformational process. You may also want to work with a therapist during this time, attend workshops, do dreamwork, to get added support, or you can form a support group in which all members work with the same material together and share their experiences.

You will not find a strictly chronological sequence to the chapter-lessons. The Myth of Childhood is not chronological as it was the first time around. Think of your myth of childhood as an organic set of impressions forming a loose pattern, a crystal of many facets which you go in and out of with your expanding consciousness. As you make progress, a growing sense of the whole will develop which is not linear but circular around a common and moving centre. We must break up the old rational ways to find a new vitality.

Statement of Purpose

We return to the childhood experience to find the traumas and splits. We re-experience these again, but this time within a healing context. We want to heal the archetypes by bringing out aspects not yet actualized or made conscious in us. We want to discover the larger pattern for our lives, and seek to fulfil it in a wholeness process. We want to live with a strong ego, a choice-making base, and also serve the larger process of the Self, the central archetype of integration and healing. We want to live the child in a non-compulsive way. We want to learn to parent ourselves without projecting out and seeking parental figures and situations. We want to find our true work in the world, and also have fulfilling relationships. We want to be centred in all that we do.

The Parents

The natural thing to do once we have contacted within us the hurt and anger repressed from childhood is to blame our parents. Yes, they were imperfect, one or more of them may have abused us, neglected us, been too hard on us, or not understood us, so wrapped up in their own big worlds were they. So we blame, we see the oppressor outside ourselves and do not look at our own self-defeating parts. But blaming others, and sometimes ourselves, does little in the way of helping us cope with life. No one is to blame for anything. Reality exists just as it is and you can do nothing to change what actually happens to you or anybody else. The facts of experience are

4

irrefutable. There is no one to blame, to make wrong in the situation. When the results are in, it is too late to change their cause. The only way to change the past is to act differently in the present. All you have is what is occurring now.

Until we have accepted our childhood just as it evolved we will be seeking causes and assigning blame. We will be hostages to fate. While we cannot change what is happening to us, we can change how we relate to what happens. This is the crucial point. Things always need to improve, to heal, everywhere. But healing comes through action, not assigning good and bad to the experiences of life, thereby rejecting one and accepting the other. To graduate into adulthood is to accept the whole and deal with it as creatively and courageously as you can while evoking the healing sources of life at the same time.

Graduating from childhood has little to do with your actual outer parents if you still have them. The only way to do it is not to change your parents but to change yourself. Your myth of childhood is inside you and this is where you must work. You cannot forgive another person for what they have done. That would be arrogance since it would imply that you have special powers. *You can, however, evoke healing for your own inner parents and children and thereby experience forgiveness yourself.* As you change, then your world will change with you. Do the inner work and the outer will change as well.

What the Myth of Childhood Is

The Myth of Childhood is the inner behavioural pattern created in actual childhood to express ourselves in adult life. We learned in childhood how to cope with fundamental experiences and how to retreat for survival. We built there a defence system to deal with potentially overwhelming forces. We had experiences of God, or a healing power, which perhaps we could not get others to understand or accept. We encountered adversarial energy in ourselves and others. We developed ego, learned self-identity. So many things happened to us. We developed and then entered the adult world.

Each of us has a story of what childhood was like. This is also our myth of childhood. It is based on selective memory and how archetypal dynamics were constellated within us. What we do now with the Transforming Childhood process is to rework the myth we developed so that the pattern can become whole, the wounded can be integrated with the wondrous, so that we can move into being a centred and effective person.

We can transform our myth of childhood. People who have gone through this process have an inspiring story to tell, and a new life to live. They will be living from their own centres rather than living governed by the original childhood material. This is a great accomplishment, one of the finest achievements possible in this lifetime. You can live and die still a child, or move fully into adult life. You have that choice.

The picture we have of childhood is the picture we have of adult life.

2 How To Use This Book

Image: *The Journal lies open – tears and laughter.*

'To become free we must re-experience the past on an inner level.'

The exercises in these lessons come out of much healing work in practising Jungian analysis, a process of helping people re-orient themselves to their own wholeness process by working through childhood material as it is still affecting them today.

You can work with the book either in therapy, in a small group or class, or on your own. What is possible is to take one chapter or lesson a week and respond to various questions. Some of the questions you will do thoroughly, some not at all. Write your responses in a journal and then share them in a small group or with a friend or therapist. It is even conceivable that a whole family can work through the book together. What an adventure that would be! If you feel overwhelmed by your material, please seek competent therapeutic help.

Methods for Transforming Childhood

In order to feel secure in dealing with childhood material as it comes up, we need to have methods for integrating the material. One of the chief methods we use is journalwork.

In journalwork we assume that much material from the unconscious can be understood and processed without having to necessarily act it out. What is essential is that we let ourselves be moved by our own experience of the archetypes in an inner and feeling way.

In letting ourselves be moved by what is being evoked, we are often reliving aspects of childhood at an archetypal level. We are not actually reliving a childhood experience, although it may feel like it. We are reliving the mythic pattern in our psyches originally created in childhood by our natural disposition, our parents and other influential people, and by the events themselves. The reliving is the re-experiencing of the archetypal pattern so that it may be changed, and so that we are not unconsciously dominated by it in adult life. Our goal is to free ourselves from the past to function creatively in the present. To become free from the past we must re-experience the past on an inner level. To become free is to take back projections originating in childhood which we put onto people and situations in the present. As adults it would be better not to go around projecting our inner child and inner parent onto our friends and authority figures.

Another value for working at an inner level is that usually we can deal with the material evoked in small enough increments so as not to be overwhelmed. Journalwork, and our other techniques, serve to process what comes up. Acting out repressed energy in the outer can lead to explosive situations which make us retreat or repress all over again.

The final level of the process is to relate the material and the changes which have taken place at an inner level to the choices we make. We move into the outer from a firm base in the inner world, where the archetypal patterns and unconscious ego-controlling attitudes lie.

In summary, you will be learning a way of working towards individuation, a wholeness process which can be applied to any area of life, dreams, relationships, and other material from one's unconscious. Our goal is to become more and more inclusive of the different elements of life by creating a growing ability to process whatever comes our way, inner and outer.

To process is everything!

3 The Methods

Image: *The vegetables lie nicely chopped on the cutting board.*

'Your journal is the true story of your life.'

The Journal

A journal is a blank book in which we write our private feelings and experiences. A journal is not a diary. In a diary, we are focused on recording a historical narrative of our lives. In journalwork, our focus is to process the energies of life by writing about them, often in a free-flowing, non-structured way. In journalwork, we are mostly concerned with the inner and consciousness-producing aspects of an experience.

Basic structures to the journalwork might include dating the entries and giving titles to most of what we write. Creating titles for things is a way of helping to realise their essence. Other structures might include researching and summarising your journal entries separately in order to create further direction from the material.

It is often best to make it clear that you want no one to read your journal without permission. If an intimate insists on reading your journal, try to get them to start one of their own. You must have the freedom to put anything you feel down on paper. Having to censor material is inhibiting to the psyche. We have enough social strictures in the outer life. We need to be freer at the inner level.

Your journal is your friend and confidant. Writing in it will also relieve you of the need to continually discuss everything with others. You will become less subject to others' influence and more contained and integrated as a person. Your journal is the true story of your life.

Specific Journalwork Techniques

• **Free Flow Writing** This is the way to write most journalwork entries. You have in mind the subject you are going to write about. You feel excited by it. But you do not usually organise how you will say it. Instead, just let the words come out. You will find that almost always you write beyond your known point of view

9

about the subject. You may also feel a sense of resolution or moving on about the problem. Date and title the entries, and work quickly and in a place where you cannot easily be disturbed.

• **Dialoguing**   This is a form of free flow writing in which you choose a part of yourself, or some energy, to have a conversation with. If, for example, you are upset with a friend, you might first go to your journal and ask the image of the friend why you feel so upset with him or her. You ask the question and then write quickly, without censoring, everything which comes into your mind. Then you might follow with another question or a feeling of your own. And so it goes until you feel you have arrived at a resolution or you have gone as far as you desire to. Such a dialogue often gives us another point of view. It opens us up to other sides of ourselves and even gives us information we may want to reject. In other words, we discover what we are projecting onto a situation or person and own it as ours. This increase in consciousness often has a resolving effect in our outer world as well.

• **The Unsent Letter**   This technique is often a powerful one and is, therefore, reserved for special occasions. Perhaps there are things, often angry things, we would like to tell another person which might be dangerous or not appropriate to say. Or we may simply feel too afraid to express our true feeling in the outer world. To our rescue comes the unsent letter. In it you write as if you were sending it. You write everything you wanted to express but thought you couldn't. Such an experience can have a freeing and resolving effect, and if truly felt, it will be as real as if you had actually sent the letter. Once you have got your feelings out, you may want to send a modified letter, more delicate and appropriate, but one still stating your position on an issue. The principle is to get the feelings out, no matter what, and this is a fairly safe way.

• **Writing Poetry**   Poetry is the language of feeling, and thus can be used to express feelings which cannot be stated appropriately otherwise. For instance, if we are experiencing intense love feelings for another person who does not reciprocate, we can still write beautiful poetry to our love object which expresses our own feelings. More often than not, we do not give them the poem. To write it is enough to get the feelings out. The journal receives our poetry and thus we do not give ourselves away. Never give yourself to someone who is not willing and able to receive you. Poetry is expressing feeling in imagery and thought. Journalwork poetry does not need to

10

conform to any literary structures. Let it flow straight from the unconscious without fear and without focusing on approval or public appreciation. Poetry is free flow writing using imagery and feeling.

• **Dreamwork**   Recording dreams with titles and dates can also be part of one's journal. After the dream report, it is helpful to write down comments. Comments may be questions or feelings about the dream, but not rational interpretations. To get to the meaning of the dream we may use various methods for re-experiencing it, which are illustrated in the *Jungian-Senoi Dreamwork Manual*. Sometimes it is possible to make connections between one's dream life and outer life. Dreams often mirror the dominant archetypal energies moving in our psyches at the time.

• **Describing Outer Life Events**   Certain events in our lives will have special significance for us, such as starting a new relationship or job. What is important here is the energy generated by the event. If I am in bed waiting for sleep, thinking over something which happened in my day, it would be important to write about it in a free flowing way until I have arrived at the essence, choice or issue involved. The goal is to process, not to merely describe. I have experienced something. What is its significance? What is its possibility? What is its danger? What is its value?

• **Active Imagination**   Active imagination, or meditative re-entry into an experience, is excellent for re-experiencing something and bringing it to resolution. We close our eyes, become quiet within ourselves, and focus on or visualise the experience. Once the flow of imagery and feeling gets going, new things which we had not anticipated may develop and move to a natural resolution of the issue. After we have lived a certain experience, we then write it down in our journal and perhaps comment on its meaning. This is often a powerful technique because, in effect, we are entering directly into our archetypal patterns, and through experiencing them, we are helping the patterns shift and become viable again instead of static and blocked. The danger is that sometimes we can become lost in the experience, and this is why writing down and processing the experience is necessary. Naturally you should not evoke more than you feel you can handle. Taking things in small doses is usually enough.

• **Changing Attitudes**   An attitude is a context out of which we make choices. Often attitudes are unconscious and can be expressed

11

as a single sentence. 'The future is likely to be worse than the present' is an attitude many of us have. Such an attitude, when not consciously realised, would cause us to make choices to avoid change and stay with the status quo, no matter what. In any situation we can observe carefully how we are acting and search for the attitudes which motivate the action. Then, once articulated, we can refashion new attitudes to be more reality oriented and less life-defeating. It is not enough to make attitudes conscious. We must also work to change them. Values are attitudes consciously realised. The more conscious we become the more choices we are able to make and the more fully and meaningfully we can live life. Once having formulated a new attitude we work with it as an affirmation. We say the new attitude to ourselves and we try it out in life by making an intention for action out of it.

• **Art Work** From time to time in order to enhance or symbolise some energy we are dealing with we can colour and draw in our journals. We are not after literal representations or beautiful art. We want only to express the energies moving in us to the best of our abilities. It is important not to negate oneself by aiming towards something one does not do well. The journal is a journey receptacle, a safe and accepting place for processing the energies of life and the psyche. Use it well.

• **Therapy and Analysis** Therapy may be needed if the material you are working with seems too evocative and more than you can safely handle. Going into therapy gives you support and insight in dealing fully with your material. The goal of most therapy is to become self-processing and integrated. Much of what we do in class or in our journals is also focused towards that end. But for especially intense experiences, or because one wants to work as deeply as possible, therapy and analysis may be the choice.

• **Enactments** Certain key experiences, not necessarily traumatic, can be enacted in long term training workshops, producing profound changes at a feeling level. This is best done with experienced trainers or therapists in a committed setting.

• **Mandala Dreamwork Training** The author's own process training using himself and associates to take people through a year's course combining dreamwork and Transforming Childhood for personal transformation. This training is also given in residential intensives (see Contact Addresses at the back of the book).

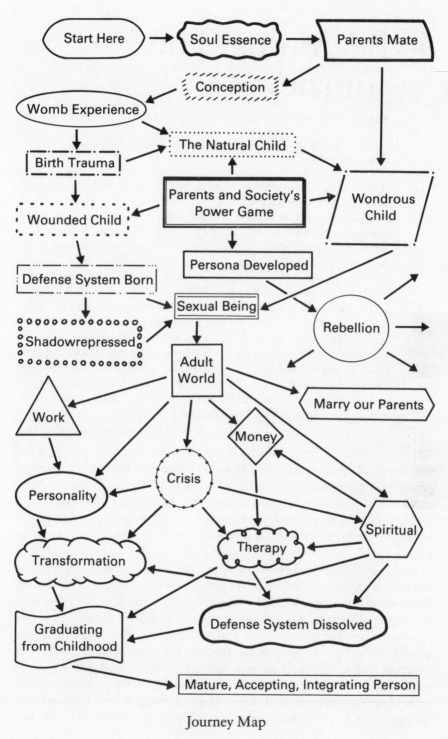

Journey Map

13

4 Beginning The Journey

Image: *The vessel.*

'...what alone is effective is a re-membering that is also a re-experiencing.'

C.G. Jung

It is of course impossible to free oneself from one's childhood without devoting a great deal of work to it ... Nor can it be achieved through intellectual knowledge only; what is alone effective is a remembering that is also a re-experiencing. The swift passage of years and the overwhelming inrush of the newly discovered world leave a mass of material behind that is never dealt with. We do not shake this off; we merely remove ourselves from it. So that when, in later years, we return to the memories of childhood we find bits of our personality still alive, which cling round us and suffuse us with the feeling of earlier times. Being still in the childhood state, these fragments are very powerful in their effect. They can lose their infantile aspect and be corrected only when they are reunited with adult consciousness. This 'personal unconscious' must always be dealt with first, that is, made conscious, otherwise the gateway to the collective unconscious cannot be opened. The journey with father and mother up and down many ladders represents the making conscious of infantile contents that have not yet been integrated.

C.G. Jung, Psychology and Alchemy, p. 62.

This passage lays the groundwork for all that we are to do. In it are the keys to dealing with childhood. These bits and pieces are of primary importance in dealing with our own psyches. Jung emphasises here the integration of the lost parts, the childhood survivors living deep in our own unconscious. If we do not reveal and integrate these parts they will cause infantile behaviour in us as adults, the clinging dependencies, strange moods, and general failures in maturity. Childhood, which one would think is to be an experience of growth and preparation for the adult years, turns out to be also an inhibitor of maturity, a liability we take into adult life. We must heal the neglected parts of ourselves as well as integrate them.

What also needs emphasis here is that we not only have the childhood story we believe in, the myth of childhood, the list of traumas and delights, but we also have the unfulfilled myth of childhood. We can return to childhood to heal and to complete the archetypes first experienced there. The end result is that what we add to Jung, to his emphasis on the trauma, is the vitality of the

14

archetypes in their fullness. We seek the Great Mother and Great Father. We seek the Wondrous Child as well as the Wounded Child. Then upon 'graduation from childhood' we will have made real a new myth. We will have found the lost parts, the full archetypes which were only partially constellated by our actual parents. We will have found life.

The Work

Respond freely in your journal to any or all of the following questions designed to help bring out the meaning for you of the above passages. There are no right responses, of course. What the questions stimulate for you as you listen to yourself is what becomes real. Write freely.

- *What does it mean to free oneself from one's childhood? Why even attempt such a task?*

- *What for you is 'a remembering that is also a re-experiencing?'*

- *Why are the memories of childhood important?*

- *What would it mean to have childhood experience lose its infantile effect?*

- *Why must we come to terms with and know our personal unconscious?*

- *What is an actual experience to go with your response to any of the above questions?*

We journey on by going back to the beginning.

15

5 The Grandparents

Image: *Roots exposed above the ground.*

'... somehow I had been taken to the door of my heritage.'

The first and last time I met my grandfather on my father's side, the old man was ninety-six and I was thirty. Two days after my father died I was taken to see my grandfather by my father's brother. He shook my hand when we met him and then briefly left the room. My uncle had said a few words about me in Yiddish to the old man which had to be translated for me. When grandfather re-entered the room he gave me a twenty dollar bill and took my hand again. I was quite moved, not by the money, but by the acceptance he seemed to be conveying towards me. The recollection of this man and this event will burn in my soul forever. I left feeling that somehow I had been guided to the door of my heritage. By this simple act I had been given the family blessing which only an elder can give. My grandfather was one who had survived a kidney operation in his own thirties at the turn of the century. Only one out of six living at that time made it through having one kidney removed. What spirit moving in this man's veins moved also in me? I wondered. With this gesture, with this blessing, I could and would do much in the world.

The Work

- *What feelings were brought out for you in reading this passage?*

- *What is a blessing?*

- *In what ways did you receive, or not receive, a blessing from your grandparents?*

- *If not a blessing, what did you receive from your grandparents?*

- *Perhaps write a letter, which you do not send, expressing your feelings about a sense of received blessing.*

- *Perhaps you could make a four-fold diagram illustrating what each of your grandparents symbolises for you.*

16

- *We may have learned a far greater sense of time from our grandparents and other family ancestors than from any clock or calendar. Write about your own sense of 'destiny time.'*

The past parents us with wisdom as the future parents us with new life.

6 Our Parents As Children

Image: *Ducks floating on a pond.*

'Children often make the best parents.'

Let us go back in time to those years before we were born. Our parents probably did not know each other then, and they were living with our grandparents most likely. As a society and a world, the environment on the material and spiritual plane would have been radically different.

Yet here we are today wondering what of that past we are still living out in an unsatisfactory way. What attitudes and values did they have which would have been appropriate then but are quite unsatisfactory now?

Picture your parents as children. What did they have to contend with? What legacy, positive and negative, were they given which they tried to pass on to you when you were a child?

I am convinced that the most universal of themes running through all childhoods is that tendency of parents to project their own repressed and otherwise unfulfilled childhood expectations onto their children. In this very real sense we were all parents to our parents' inner child. We found ourselves in a fundamental conflict between bringing up their unresolved child and affirming and expressing our own natural child, the person we were meant to be.

What then is it that we most have to forgive our parents for? Obviously the traumas and neglects, but perhaps most cogently for the enormous amount of time and effort spent in trying to make of us the child they always wanted to be and never were. The only real wound that any of us carry is the wound of lost life which can never be gained again and therefore must be given over as a loss into the fires of redemption. The irony lies in the realisation that what the parents tried to give us in their own best expectations was in fact a loss for us.

Perhaps we feel we never conformed to the parents' expectations by rebelling against the pressure. Yet even while we created distance, in the unconscious we remained as tied as ever. We remained tied in reaction rather than conformity. The true freedom is to find ones own individual way, the way from the natural child to the adult we were meant to be.

The Work

- *What am I holding on to that I haven't forgiven my parents for?*

- *What is one of the most vivid images of my parents' childhood? What images of my parents as children do I have? What inner image of parent inside me does this evoke?*

- *What are some attitudes towards life that my parents may have developed as children?*

- *Visualise yourself holding your parent as a child in your arms. What feelings are created?*

- *Were your parents forgiving or not forgiving of their parents? In what way has this affected you?*

- *Describe how you might have been the parent to your parent's inner child.*

- *In what way could you still be parenting your parent's inner child today?*

The child is parent to us all.

7 Our Evolutionary History

Image: *A luminous dark sphere shadowed with light.*

'You are not yet born, yet something is already here, an immense complexity, a miracle of billions of births.'

Picture it yourself. Before you were born the great organism, life, was already here on this planet. Each one of us is made up of actual molecules, the same type of basic units of matter which also helped compose other living creatures centuries and centuries ago. We exist with a consciousness built out of tens of thousands of years work and experience by *homo sapiens*, man and woman.

The legacy of what we call life is in us today, but far more than we as single individuals can be. The whole evolutionary history of who we are exists now in each of us, and yet together we are one great organism living, moving, changing on this earth in order to produce the essence which will evolve the next generation a step further along than we are at present.

Think of it and marvel. How petty our troubles are when we consider the immensity of the achievement which is ours to live today.

Will we embrace life and make our contribution to the whole?

You are coming to this planet which already has life. You are not yet born, yet something is already here, an immense complexity, a miracle of billions of births. You are but one potential in many; you will be arriving soon. Think of it. You will be next one day.

What will you bring with you? What will you find already here on this planet earth? What will you contribute by the time you exit life?

The worlds are spinning closer. Welcome what will soon be your ground, your resting place, your state of manifestation. Welcome the great essential we call life!

The Work

- *Read the paragraph over, perhaps out loud. Let yourself feel it. Go into meditation or visualisation. Be there somewhere in the universe. Who are you at this point? What are you coming to?*

- *After your experience, please write it up, giving feelings, images and so on, and responding to the questions embodied in the text.*

- *List the possibilities which come to mind as you begin to feel the spark of what could be and enter into a journey of receiving a body which is born and goes through childhood into adulthood.*

- *And, of course, list any hesitations, resistances or questions you might have. After all, part of you might not want to be born.*

To evolve is to step through time into time.

8 The Conception

Image: *The flame has left its fire.*

'Self born of what and born to what?'

In an instant something of you was present somewhere, somehow. In the dark warm depth of human flesh a whole lot of energy was at work expanding itself and gathering in.

And where was soul, that infinitesimal spark which is neither flesh nor energy? The moment of essence into being must have been the moment, indeed. Nothing begets nothing and something is born. What great rivers of life and destiny met in that uniting which your parents made and created together in their time of pleasure?

Seen from a more cosmic viewpoint, two great energies had their meeting, the masculine and the feminine, and out of that coming together the Self was born. Self born of what and born to what?

Not all seed reaches an egg. One does and the penetration is done. Swift multiplication follows, matter quickens within incredible possibility. And clinging there to warm and nurturing flesh, the wall of the womb, the supplier of what it takes to become. The cost is everything. The commitment is total. There is often no turning back.

The Work

- *How would you describe the moment of conception as you think it happened for you?*

- *What was the nature of your parent's union? Was it spontaneous and joyful, or ambivalent and strained? Were they united in spirit as well as in flesh?*

- *What effect, if any, do you imagine the quality of your parents' union had on your entry into life?*

- *How would you describe the two streams of life which came together when your parents united, conceiving you?*

- *How would you describe your soul, or spiritual essence, at the time of your conception? Just let go and describe. We are*

22

admittedly reaching into the unknown, not for literal facts, but for archetypal flow.

- *How would you describe your womb environment during those first days of rapid growth?*

- *Do you in any way regret being conceived? Do you have any regrets about the union of the parents that conceived you? What are they?*

We are conceived within the womb of time to break out into eternity.

Conceiving the Child

9 The Womb

Image: *The fisherwoman has caught a silver fish.*

'Limitation is true freedom'

Something happened to you back then when you were still in the womb. What was it? Try to recall.

Or if you wish to remain in the present, ask yourself, what is the womb of your life right now? How do you deal with constriction and any narrowing of your personal freedom? Do you rebel and kick and try to fight your way out? Or do you accept your fate and go with whatever is happening to you?

Are you womb-cursed or womb-blessed?

Somewhere back then in the deep recesses of the bellied womb of flesh of your mother, you met and dealt with the first closing in on you. Picture yourself in the first three months of growth, a floating ball in the warm pond of your own amniotic sack. As you grow you reach the walls, the natural restrictions which are the structures of your own mother's womb.

You must curl and almost contract, yet continue growing, continue pushing out at all sides so that you can continue to manifest yourself. And the pushing and the stretching become more difficult, until one day the walls of your life begin contracting and you find yourself being squeezed out.

How well do you take restriction today? Limitation is true freedom!

The Work

- *Visualise yourself in your mother's womb. Take a few minutes with eyes closed to let go to the feeling and possible images. What is the experience like? How are you responding?*

- *What is your personal history of becoming dizzy? When does it seem to happen? What feelings are evoked from becoming nauseous? What can you do about it? What change of perspective is needed?*

- *What areas in your present life need containing? What is containment and how does it work as a process?*

- *What relation to the womb experience might commitment have?*

- *In what ways could limitation be true freedom for you? How can limitation free you to become yourself?*

The womb of commitment is the place for new birth.

10 Meditative Re-entry into the Birth Experience

The following meditation is for use in going through the conception and birth experience again. This may be done in a group with the leader or instructor saying the words meditatively, or individually by first recording the meditation and then listening to it as you go through your own experience. The meditative re-entry into the mythic birth experience helps heal your original encounter way back in childhood. Our fundamental concept here is that childhood still lives in us as adults as The Myth of Childhood. We return to the myth consciously to re-experience it once again and to transform it. Once transformed this makes a difference in how we live our lives. For the myth itself is the archetypal pattern still there controlling us in all that we do whether we know it or not. The re-entry, when it profoundly moves us, changes the pattern. You may or may not be moved depending on, among other things, your ability to let go and go with the experience. Some people have had a lot of guided imagery and so have become dulled to being spontaneously moved by authentic imagery. They have learned to control the image just as they control concepts. When you stay in control as ego you cannot be evoked by the archetype, the deeper bedrock of the unconscious. It is better to let go then.

For the sceptics who do not believe that childhood still lives in them archetypally we have only to look at how we all wake up in the morning. For the way we wake to the day is the way we were born. If you were severely traumatised then you will not like waking each morning. You may not even like falling asleep. If you do not come into your day remembering dreams and other thoughts from the night, then your birth transition was abrupt as well as traumatic. These statements are suggestions about symbolism involved. They make sense to many people. Look for yourself and compare your sleep-waking pattern with what you know or imagine of your birth. We want to change all that, not rationally, but by completing the archetype.

All births have some trauma in them. They would not be initiation rites otherwise. But only trauma, bright lights, coldness, lack of warm skin, lack of contact with the mother and father, being slapped, not wanted, dropped, strangled by having the umbilical cord cut too soon, and so on, is one-sided in terms of birth. Where also is the love, the spiritual halo around the mother and the room, the quiet, the calm, the joy, the sensitivity, the warm body to cling to, the nurturing breast, the smiles, the care? All this needs to be included in the birth process also. And a possible warning to those who are trying these days to make childbirth simply wonderful and easy, as with birthing in water. We come into this world needing challenge and difficulty, yes, even from the beginning, as well as nurturing and ease. Be aware of the opposites and keep both present. Dealing with reality as it is, not as you would like it to be, is the principle.

For the meditative experience of being born allow yourself one to two hours. The meditative experience itself could take forty-five minutes to an hour. Then there is time to process, to write about it, and to share with others, making the experience conscious as well as feeling it deeply. It takes place lying comfortably on the floor, not to fall asleep, but to be deeply relaxed. If you fall asleep you are resisting, you are letting yourself fall into the unconscious, so great is the original trauma. You may need to do this, but if you can, resist sleep and remain actively aware. There should be pauses between statements so that people have time to let their images and feelings come up. This is not an exercise dictating what to see on the inner plane, as so many visualisation exercises are. So now begin! The separate paragraphs indicate pauses of a minute or two for people to have their own experiences enough so that they develop fully, yet not too long or they will go somewhere else or move ahead. The leader's eyes are also closed to better sense what is happening in everyone – unless, of course, you have to read the following.

The Meditative Re-entry

'Please find a comfortable place on the floor. You may lie on your back or on your side in a more foetal position. If you have to, sit up, but will this be a relaxed enough position from which to go deeply? This next forty-five minutes or so we will be letting go to an inner process. Through the meditative state we will be able to go back to the original experience as it has been implanted into our psyche, go back and also go through it again for healing. Most, if not all of us, have had a traumatic birth experience, and this affects us still today. So is everybody comfortable with eyes closed. I will be aware as leader and if it becomes too much for anyone just come out of your meditation, and if you have to leave the room, do so.

'Letting your body be relaxed, let go to inner spaces. Let your breathing clear out a space in which nothing is. Breathe it through, opening up to the inner space, and letting go of distractions. They can still be there but outside the space you are opening. Let go also of ego concerns, still the mind, no inner commenting now, no abstractions or analysing, just let go and be, let go and let happen. Time to go with, and be present at, a mystery which may or may not develop for you.

'Where are you now? It seems that this is before your conception, before you were a body here on this earth. Somewhere out there, somewhere out there, just feel – see that sense of universe before birth.

'Is there a presence there? What is your first impression? Stay with it, however fleeting.

'And now finding that spot, that point, that presence which is you, can you sense yourself as present to a larger universe even before birth? You know nothing of earth yet.

'But now your focus is being drawn somewhere. Do you sense it as a pull or what?

'Now something is happening. Are you ready, or almost ready?

'You are being drawn now to energy being formed, sensing even before you exist as body two other bodies at work on each other, energy and rhythm, substance, being drawn, being drawn in. Are you being pulled in or asking to come in to their embrace, to be right there in the middle of that great energy?

'How are they making love now? What do you sense? Let go to it, for you are to be there.

'Be ready now. How do you sense yourself and their presence, their union creating you, the moment. Let the moment of your creation come as you let go to it, the energy, the expansion the contraction, the moment. Experience it!

'Now you are energy in flesh, what does it feel like? See your cells multiplying, your embryo form floating in a mother sea and attached to her womb wall. Stay with that for a moment. See, feel it, let yourselves be present to it. What do you experience in yourself? What do you experience is happening outside yourself?

'But we can't stay there forever. You are growing and growing, the cells multiplying, the sense of your own being even greater. Is anything left of what you had before you became body? What's it like to be in the mother womb at around three months now?

'And then you keep growing, that never seems to stop, your floating sea is smaller as you bump the walls of the womb, as it touches and surrounds you into the middle months, feeling those middle months. Sense it now, be there, do you not like it or not?

'Tighter now, the embryo you is getting so big and feeling the tightness of mother womb growing about you. Can you make sounds, even push and kick, what are you doing there now? What is the quality of your being, the feel of it as you react to the tightening, the squeezing all about you?

'And what voices do you hear from out there? Take a moment to sense the activity out there even if you do not yet know the words for it.

'Ah, the squeezing, the tightness, you are so big in your womb nest. How is it? What new feelings are there in you? Sensing the next necessary event. The time is coming, is it here already? No, you are not ready? You don't want to be born yet, or you do want to be born? So many feelings!

'Who initiates the task, you as baby, or your mother? Now waves are happening, the contractions, the squeezes, and your reaction, are you ready yet to take the head-first plunge, or is it a different position for you with unusual things happening? Let it come now. The moment – The Moment is almost here.

'It is here now. The birth. Go! Arrive! Time waits for no one!

'What sounds? What light? What presences come in at you? Let go to them. This is your birth as it originally happened. It is happening to you now. Let it happen, yet react to it in your own way. What are you feeling?

'Where are you now? What do you sense? – feel? Relaxed? Tense? Cared for? Loved? Hurt? Initiated? What about the others in the place where you are and have never been before? What about the others?

Resting now, staying with your experience, perhaps some of you can share just a bit, what comes to you, an essence from right where you are. Describe what you are feeling right now. Make it conscious if you can.'

There may not be much sharing. We want people to stay in their meditative state because we will be asking them soon to go through the birth again, but in the best way possible for them. When working in a group, ask for a few responses here, both to wake up those who may have fallen asleep, and to give everyone a sense of what has happened. This lasts only about five minutes as a few people speak briefly. Do not comment or enter into dialogue with what they say. Just elicit personal revelation.

Second Meditative Re-entry

'Now again with eyes closed we have a chance this time to go through our birth experience the way we would have liked it, not perfectly, but a full experience with plenty of love and sensitivity there as well.

'Again, see, feel, yourself out there in the universe somewhere, a presence before birth, before body, before parents even. You are present in the more transcendent, your essence only, what is it like? What is your essence there?

'Do you sense a purpose and destiny drawing you? Do you want to come into the body this time? Are you ready, as ready as you can be? What is attracting you?

'Allow yourself to move towards the conception now, see the energy focused somewhere, the parents in their physical essence moving together, generating the child to be, you. Do they know it, welcome you, want you? And do you want them?

'Now let it happen! You are conceived and growing rapidly as flesh. Feel it! What is it like? Let it happen.

'And where are you? Sense your own presence within a larger presence, the mother-womb, the shaking, the movement, the warmth, the sounds, the sea in which you float and swim.

'Sense yourself growing, physically and in awareness. What do you experience now as the months go by and the womb closes in on you? Let it happen, keep letting things happen.

'Now in that last month, how is it all, and what is your mood? How open, how adventuresome do you feel yourself to be? What purpose has seized you as you prepare for entry into this world and this life? Are you helping things to happen? Are things happening to you?

'Let the contractions begin! Now the labour, the change, the

31

initiation rite, the transition. Experience it fully, go through it and feel.

'That part of you coming out now. Even as it is happening let your body there on the floor move to it, the contractions, the squeezes, the noises, the mother sounds and the embryo to baby sounds. Let your body express all that it is sensing and feeling, as you let go to the journey movement now.

'And then the opening and the birth. The Birth!

'What is the response you are receiving this time, the mother, the father, energy, the healers present, the sounds, the light and the darkness, the things going right and the things going a bit wrong. Still the birth in fullness, the wanted birth. Do you want it now? Do they want it now? Yes, let go to it and experience the wholeness of the event. The Wholeness!

'What comes upon you now? What do you need? Are you being fed? The newness of it all. The sensations on your skin and in your body. See the images. See her. See him. See yourself. Look! Really look. Really sense. Describe for yourself to yourself the experience.

'And now resting quietly, knowing that you have been through a lot, just be there within yourself. No one will ask you to come out of that deep place just yet. That is yours to be with, to cherish, to come to terms with. Let the images, the thoughts, the feelings flow, as your psyche wants them to.

'Now recall a little and compare, begin making conscious your process. Yes, it's hard to come back from such a deep place, but you will have to sometime. See if you can begin to do it now. Slowly but with focus. Compare perhaps the two births, the contrasts. What new happened for you the second time through?

'What new healing may have taken place? What new purpose?

'We are making conscious the process now as a way of transition, of getting to the essence and acknowledging also the process.

'Would some of you like to share a few words, a feeling, or just describe the images, not the whole thing, but part of what moved you?'

In groupwork, sensitive discussion probably follows with participants saying a few things. You as leader can do a little question-asking and resaying of significant statements. But not too much. It is their experience we are after, not yours! Gradually people will open their eyes and come out of it. If this does not seem to be happening, then instruct them to slowly come back to this reality, open their eyes, look around and ground themselves again here in this world. Then ask them to write in their journals for a few minutes about the experience. Then have some sharing around the circle without comment from others or yourself. Then link hands in a circle as the closing and leave. Ask for a full write up of the experience to be handed in at the beginning of the next session.

You as leader need also to process what happened for you. Either go through the process yourself after the session, even right after while the energy is fresh, and when everyone else has gone home. What have you learned from all this? How have you changed?

Birth

11 Choosing Your Parents

Image: *A tree split open by a great force.*

'We must accept what happens to us rather than resist it.'

We come into this world a mere speck of flesh and a spark of soul in somebody's body. We have not chosen to be there. Our mother and father have sex and the sperm and egg come together to produce the me that is I. Did I want to be here? Did I ask to be chosen? Did I have any choice in the quality of the parents I received? Was this all accident or is there some destiny in it?

If you asked me why I chose my parents I would first say I had no choice in the matter. But if you pressed me to reflect further I would have to reply, yes, I must have chosen those particular parents because no one in their right mind would have given me the people I got. My choice-making was strange indeed. Certainly God could not have made such a choice, so I must have made it myself.

Why did I choose my parents?

I wanted to make life difficult for myself. I came into the world as a very strong person to have given myself such difficult parents. I was sent away to boarding school at the age of six because they both decided that they were not fit to be parents, and that poetry and art were their only devotion. To compound the event, I was told by my father's girlfriend after my mother's death that he said he had not had sex with my mother for the first ten years of their marriage, and that I was an accident.

So I must have chosen my parents riding a stream of destiny so strong that it demanded they should have sex. I look on in disbelief at the precariousness of life. It might just as well have been someone else who was born in our place but somehow we were meant to be here.

No matter the tragedy, or the goodness of childhood, we can face the question, why did I choose my parents? Why those two? Why was it necessary to have those parents? The transformation of childhood is the acceptance of childhood just as it is. In therapy I discovered rage at what had been done to me, but what could I do but express it and let it go? Childhood was over for me. I had only the charged and tragic memories. These also I would have to work through. For to hold on to the tragedy of the past is to remain blocked to the future as well.

One great lesson of life is to accept rather than resist what happens to us. I would have preferred better parents to the ones I had. But now, years later I have got over my rejection of them. They are my parents, quaint, abusive, but essential to my destiny. I do not want someone else's parents as I did in my youth. There is a peculiar, wonderful quality about these parents of mine.

I have accepted reality.

I have chosen my parents.

The Work

- *Why did your parents choose you?*

- *Why did you choose your parents? Write freely about how you played a part in receiving the parents you got. What is it about your particular set of parents which is necessary to the fulfilment of your own life?*

- *Why was it necessary for you to be born? Why is it necessary to live?*

- *Create a little humour about the fact that you were born to the parents you have got. Tell someone about it, or act it out a bit for a group.*

Through choice we turn fate into destiny.

12 Nurturing

Image: *Her breasts are bare.*

'No one will give us all the love we feel we need in this life.'

How well and how fully were you nurtured, fed and warmed after your birth? While suckling on the full breast and clinging to the ground of your mother's flesh, what stability and openness were born there?

Or was it more the opposite for you? Did you experience yourself taken away or deprived of the breast and the holding? Did you experience also the void and the coldness of the Dark Mother of Deprivation?

> There is a photograph of me as a baby in a nappy standing on my mother's lap. One of her arms steadies me while the other arm and hand hold a baby bottle. My mother is well dressed and sophisticated. My down-to-earth aunt, her sister, is also in the picture, as well as my girl cousin. Obviously my slim mother did not define herself as a breast-feeder and so I missed out on some essential nurturing. I know now what it is like to suckle on a warm woman's breast, to feel secure in letting go to a basic need, to experience the relief of someone actually being there willingly for me, someone who enjoys giving to me. What a fight it must have been struggling with that bottle, my first civilised tool to manipulate, cold impersonal thing that it was, even if the cow's milk was warm inside it. I had to learn in adult relationships with caring women that nurturing was not something you could manipulate to get. I had to become the vulnerable baby again before she could give freely to me. At first it felt humbling. Now I experience it as a natural letting go to receiving and pleasure. I am receiving. I am being nurtured by something real!

Take this moment as the Womb of the Now. How fully do you give and receive nurturing? Are you a compulsive seeker of nurturing? Or a compulsive giver unable to receive? If so, what unfulfilled needs from childhood still hide in your unconscious?

Most adults seek and express nurturing in relationships. But what may be crucial is to become more and more self-nurturing to oneself.

No one will give us all the love we feel we need in this life. The answer is to love! And to love oneself.

The Work

- *What feelings do you have from reading the above passage?*

- *What questions from the above would be important for you to respond to? What is your response?*

- *Enter a meditative state and feel-imagine yourself at your mother's breast. How long can you stay there and experience whatever comes up? What is it like? Write about it.*

- *Look at your present relationships in terms of the wish to nurture others. Explore ways this can be done and the values and consciousness involved.*

- *Look also at your present relationships as places to be nurtured, to let go to warmth and acceptance, and to be fed.*

And we shall be nurtured by choice, not plenty.

13 Bonding

Image: *A bird flies into the sun.*

'And in love-making, are we not again yielding to the primal bond?'

Bonding is the mandala, the completing and breaking circle of life. We are born and immediately we seek to cling, to be reunited with the mother-flesh, the nurturing warmth of the primal source out of which we so recently came. And in love-making, are we not again yielding to the primal bond? So many of us find it hard to let go of a relationship when it has ended. The beloved is again the parent and we are again the child. We are required by reality to leave the mother bond but we fight it. We are afraid to be alone, to exist solitary to ourselves.

Witness the toddler of one and a half, moving a room away from the parent and then hurriedly returning. Leave the door open, Daddy. Don't break the bond on me.

In life we bond to all sorts of things. We bond to our cigarettes if we are a smoker. To our lovers and friends for support. To our work and our jobs for security. Life is all so simple when we look at it from a child's point of view. But as adults we are not here to live a child's life, at least not all the time. All experiences of pleasure, in fact, may be in some significant way a return to childhood. The adult needs the primal experiences but does not need to be bound by them.

It sometimes takes willingness to step through the fire. The tiny child crawls away from its parent to explore the world. After all, there is more than mother in life. But should the distance feel too great and the bond too thin, then the child cries out to be reunited with its parents. It has gone forward but retreated again. And so it is with us adults. We need the warmth and renewal of the bond and the love object. But we do not need the attachment. It is good to have little attachment left by the end, to become individuals with the parental dynamics inside us. We then have the primal bonding in us as a healing circle in which we are integrating all our parts. The inner family is alive, and as adults we do not need to compulsively seek primary bonding in outer family or groups. We are individuating. We are developing wholeness within.

The Work

- *With your eyes closed see yourself as a small child relating to a parent. What bonding pattern shows up? How does this pattern also assert itself in your present life? What creative choices might you make regarding your bonding pattern?*

- *If you at times feel isolated and cold, what are some conscious ways you can experience bonding with some source of renewal? Explore creative bonding experiences which are not self-destructive or compulsive. Compulsive eating, sexuality, drug taking, talking or smoking reflect unconscious bonding behaviour. Loving someone, relating to animals, having massage and bodywork done on you are more conscious ways to find renewal through bonding.*

- *Also practise unbonding from compulsive needs. Use your will to break compulsive habits and deal with the anxiety which is evoked. Give yourself so much love and affirmation that the compulsive need to bond will diminish. The overweight person is often one who feels afraid and incapable of being loved or bonded to. Gorging on food becomes less compulsive when we love ourselves and become feeling-sensitive to our bodies. Loving our bodies means feeling and healing them.*

We can bond with others if we have formed a healing bond within.

14 The Baby as Body

Image: *The walled city has some houses on fire.*

'We must therefore liberate the body as well as the soul.'

The body is where we live. It is the house we inhabit. But how many of us totally accept this house we carry with us? It is the source and bedrock of all our adventures. We cannot escape it for very long. This body of ours has a language of its own. We need to come to terms with where we live.

The baby is being born, the baby is having sensations within the womb and then out of the womb. What care does that helpless body receive immediately and in the future?

Babies have bodies. Bodies need plenty of touching and hugging and having needs met. Bodies need food and flexibility. Immediately the body has needs of its own and the baby cries out. But even at the start so many parents oppose the natural rhythms of the body. Feeding time four times a day. Let the baby cry. Be afraid to carry the baby around with you everywhere.

The new baby who receives plenty of physical attention will grow up with an attitude that its needs can and will be met in a plentiful world. Strength comes out of being given to, as well as from giving.

The list is long of all the major body experiences we go through as a child. Birth ... breast or bottle feeding ... bowel movements ... falling down and experiencing pain ... eating ... defecating; being washed ... masturbating ... hugging ... experiencing anger ... seeing oneself in the mirror ... male and femaleness ... sickness ... vitality and high energy ... feeling others with warm bodies also.

So much of early life is felt through the body, and then in the adult years we experience all sorts of physical symptoms as we deal with the stresses and changes of life. It is as if each one of us has had our bodies rigidly patterned to act in set ways to life's problems. And, like so many things, the original patterning was formed early in childhood. Watch for it. When do I become sick and what kind of sickness do I get?

Much sickness, from the serious to the mild, from allergies to cancer, from the common cold to flatulence, are due to the original body-reaction pattern formed in childhood. The remedy? Try consciousness and change. Discover for yourself the original pattern producing the present symptoms. Try to restructure the childhood reactive pattern to a more natural and vital functioning. Every one of us could gain from extensive bodywork of one sort or another. Have we been held lovingly enough as children? Are we trying in adult life to make of sex the healer for the traumatised body it was never meant to be?

A basic premise flows through all the childhood material. We are our bodies. Our symptoms in adult life are evoked by contemporary stresses, but their origin is in the body-reactive pattern formed early in childhood. We must therefore liberate the body as well as the soul. We must liberate the life force physically as well as mentally.

The Work

- *List the typical body symptoms you regularly suffer in adult life. They do not have to be major, and can include such simple things as backaches and warts. Now for each symptom associate, or let flow, early childhood memories and images. What are your earliest experiences of having a body? Write these down. Let things flow freely.*

- *Draw a body chart of yourself, and at various parts of your body place on the symptoms you have or now suffer from. Where do you seem to feel most vulnerable? Where are the areas of greatest vitality? Write steps you will take to deal with the troubled parts of your body, such as exercise and other forms of healing.*

Your body is reality.

15 Waking

Image: *A ball of fire growing in intensity.*

'What is done in the beginning sets the course for what comes after.'

The way we wake up each morning can be the way we were born into the world, whether we have a memory of that first entrance or not.

Consider your life and how you start your day. Do you wake eager to experience the newness of each day? Or do you tend to return to sleep as the much preferred place to be? Why face the world any sooner than we have to? The warmth of the bed and the unknown land of the unconscious may seem preferable to the suffering, excitement and choice-making of an active day. Do you jump out of bed into the day's activities too soon, or do you take a few moments to savour and acknowledge the transition between sleep and waking?

How many of us wake each morning eager to face and fulfil life to the utmost? How many of us bring with us into the day a dream from the night, making transition from the world of moon to the world of sun? If our transition is poor from sleep to waking, chances are that the transition from mother-womb life to separate life in the world was difficult and abrupt.

Many people are afraid to fall asleep at night and eat anxiously before bed or read a book. After sleep they have to fight to get up, they have to have a jarring radio or alarm clock to wake them up. Truly, their basic life patterns were traumatised at birth and still affect them daily in waking life.

What would it mean for each of us to wake slowly each morning capturing a dream or a significant thought or feeling? What would it mean to wake refreshed and eager to leave bed and deal with the joys and trials of a typical day? It is crucial that we begin each day at the beginning, not somewhere partly down the road. What is done in the beginning sets the course for what comes after. If you are not starting each day significantly, look at your present sleeping and waking pattern and create a more fulfiling one. Each day that we wake fully and consciously is a day in which we transform a little more the traumatic entry of our original birth experience.

It is time to wake up. It is time to get it together, to grow, to change, to become vital. Choose and move!

Dream Time

The Work

- *What exactly is your sleeping and waking pattern? Describe in detail and then relate it to how you feel you were originally born. Do you wake inwardly focused or outwardly focused? Do you wake thinking of a dream, or some outer task you have to do that day? Or do you wake resistantly, wanting to hide or go back to sleep.*

- *In what ways have you woken up to life and its meaning? In what ways might you still be asleep?*

- *What does it mean to wake to life? Ask this of yourself and a few friends this week.*

- *Write in your journal for a week on how you seem to wake up and the changes you are making in that pattern.*

Those first must sleep who would awake.

16 The Pain of Childhood

Image: *The tree's branch has been broken.*

'We are not yet mature if we always seek pleasure over pain.'

'Johnny, you shouldn't hit Tommy. That's not good.'
'Janie, be nice to your younger sister. She loves you. It's not nice to yell at your sister. See, you made her cry.'
Behind each of these typical statements used in child upbringing are certain attitudes.

- It's wrong to hurt people.

- The right thing to do is to make people feel good. You would want them to do that for you, wouldn't you?

Who gives us these attitudes? Do they come directly through us in our own wisdom, or are they imposed on us from outside? The answers seem obvious. The reality of the situation is that children in their natural state fight as well as play together, inflict pain on each other as well as make each other feel good. And what do parents do with their children? None of them would consider it good behaviour, but all parents cause pain in their children. If they could only admit that they are inflicting pain as well as pleasure on their children, the parents of the world would become a lot more realistic about life.

Pain is here to stay. We have pain receptors built into our bodies just as we have pleasure centres. We are taught to avoid pain and seek pleasure, but is this a valid approach to life? Perhaps, just perhaps, there is just as much to learn from suffering as there is from pleasure.

Where our training in childhood falls down is in being taught that pleasure, the good, the socially acceptable, the pleasant, are all of value, while pain, suffering, weirdness, wildness, rebelliousness, are all roundly condemned as being bad.

Is it any wonder that we have not been trained to deal with the difficult side of life? We have been taught to repress the bad in favour of the good. Look to your own past. What was your earliest experience of pain? What brought it about? Were you taught how to deal with it?

A new mature attitude regarding pain is that pain is as valid as pleasure in living a meaningful life.

We are not yet mature if we always seek pleasure over pain. There is pleasure when the life force flows freely, when we feel healthy, when things are working well in life. There is pain when the life force is being blocked, when there is resistance to change, when things are unbalanced or needing to be destroyed. Pain is also the effect resulting from the challenge to let go of the old and bring in the new. If these statements destroy a few attitudes, let them. If you are angry now or agitated, it may be because some of your own attitudes are at stake. Let go and go with. Learn from the new even if it embodies the dark side of life.

In compassion we can feel the overwhelming pain we must have felt back there in childhood. We are all born into a rough life, and somehow the 'wounded one' lurks waiting, hoping to be rescued. Yet nobody comes. We must leave our hiding places ourselves and go out to where healing and truth can occur. Yes, there is an infinite well of sorrows, and sometimes my own hurting dips down into a universal despair. This makes me very sad, but my sadness is real. I welcome the pain of being real. No, I am not always happy and don't need to be. Wholeness is better than happiness any day, and when my pain comes I will be ready for it.

I know that within pain are the fires of my own transformation.

The Work

- *Return to the most painful experience of your childhood and write about it. What you will be doing is accepting pain as a natural ingredient of life that originally you closed off to. Now open and let it happen.*

- *Work with pain in your life, not as 'pain' but as 'energy.' Energy is the sense of movement within and without, which creates new life. You feel pain. Focus on it directly. Find it in your body, seek images from it, look at your reactions to it, and above all, recall early childhood memories and attitudes which now relate to your pain. Pain immediately plunges us right back there into childhood.*

- *List your attitudes towards pain. Revise each one to make them more realistic and accepting.*

There are things which only pain will teach us.

17 Anger

Image: *The well has been blocked.*

'It takes energy to repress energy.'

We are only ultimately angry at ourselves. Even though it feels as if we are angry at everyone else who has ever hurt us, ultimately the anger we feel is our own.

We become angry when we feel powerless and vulnerable to being hurt. Normally, our defence system prevents negative energy from getting through to our consciousness. But every so often someone 'presses our buttons', the attack penetrates our defensive pattern, and repressed energy sizzles us to the core.

It takes energy to repress energy. To protect our wound we become angry, and to protect our self-image, we repress the anger. This causes an energy drain which devitalises us and creates depression and despair. Thus by freeing and transforming our anger pattern we free the life energy from the defence system. To free our anger we first identify the defence system that may be keeping us from experiencing it. Then we express our anger. Anger is one of the two great instinctive forms of energy expression, the other is sex. Finally, we transform our anger by allowing ourselves to feel the wound underneath it. We must freely experience the ecstasies of suffering as well as of pleasure.

Now let us look at the nature of our defence system. At some point in childhood we chose to hide our emotions and feelings from ourselves, and others. We were confronted by the overwhelming power of the parents, other significant authority figures, or a traumatic event. We could not take it, so we constructed a defence system to hide from ourselves and to deny the full impact of reality.

As adults this defence system no longer works as well as it worked in childhood. In fact, it imprisons us from living fully. We may deny aspects of reality, space out, identify with archetypes, roles and religions, rationalise feelings, repress feelings, avoid intense situations and the next life developments. You name it, we have all done it under the aegis of protecting ourselves.

What is there to protect ourselves from? It is all life. Reality is what exists, so why not encompass all of it?

48

We return emotionally to our myth of childhood simply because that is where it all started. We go back to the traumas and grand hurts to face our adversaries, to re-experience these events emotionally without closing off this time. By suffering through the trauma without becoming completely defensive we will be helping the underlying patterns and attitudes to transform, so that we may regain our life energy and direction.

Yes, it's painful. But pain is an energy that one can learn to handle. Suffering exists and is essential to life, so why not accept it emotionally and create with it?

The Work

- *What was your anger like in childhood? How is it similar to, or different from, your adult expression of anger?*

- *Try and describe a wounding experience, where the pain became too much, in childhood. Relive it at some level using journalwork. Perhaps you could write it out. Or write unsent letters describing your feelings. Or paint the scene? Or keep telling friends about your trauma until you, yourself, have accepted it? Or enact it in a group?*

- *How would you describe your defence system in terms of anger? Write an affirmation accepting your own anger. Formulate an intention to express your anger more creatively.*

To wield the sword you must first draw it from its safe scabbard.

18 Witches

Image: *The tree is hollow.*

'... the dark witch, the one familiar with evil ...'

When I was a child in boarding school, we would spend the summers in the school camp far away in the woods. It was always a highlight for we eleven-year-old boys to receive twenty-five cents and take a hike all day to the honey man. We climbed and ran through the forest and then descended by a track to a small wooden house which still had a water mill wheel working in the stream. This 'white witch' was an old man surrounded by his swarms of bees and his many bee hives. He seemed stooped over, not from suffering, but from being some sort of guardian of the waters and caretaker of the bees. To us he was magic, and therefore to be feared. Bees meant danger as we ran barefooted through the fields of wild flowers. But this man who lived alone had some influence he could use to make bees give their best.

We each paid our twenty-five cents and received a whole honeycomb of our very own. The 'white witch' was for me the one who knew nature and who had been moulded by her. The price he paid was his old age, and the gain he received from his worker bees was the elixir, the sweetest, most powerful essence of natural life.

The world itself was a lot duller the next day. But something beyond the everyday remained in our imaginations forever. The White Witch had created in small, growing boys a fearful and excited respect for the natural forces of life.

I had my terrible witches also. My own mother was one, brooding in bed when I came home on short vacations each year. Those gleaming eyes hid their sadness, but revealed, all too clearly, a wildness to the young boy – myself. This woman held immense power over my mind and destiny, and I slowly learned to placate her when I could. Alas, she followed me into my dreams and secret thoughts, terrorising me for years. She was to me the dark witch, the one familiar with evil who used it on me and justified her every action. I learned from her the truth, which she herself did not seem to face, that there is no escape from the pain of consciousness, and that the darkness of the night is too often laced with despair.

Now, I know her to be my mother, old, neurotic Gene Derwood

Williams, who had been in the mental hospital for a year when I was three.

The Work

- *What feelings, or moods, are aroused for you by this passage?*

- *Why not describe the experience of a 'witch' in your own childhood? 'Witches' seem to represent the magical, sometimes evil and sometimes nature-power side of things. What effect did your witch experiences have on you then?*

- *In present life, see if you can recall an experience of a 'witch', someone with numinous or archetypal power over you. This might be a real person or someone from your dreams.*

- *How do you express, or not express, the witch side of yourself? Look for the more irrational and bizarre behaviour which yet has a strange logic, a secret meaning, to it. Perhaps this witchy part is a peculiarity of your own mental state or consciousness? Could that be?*

- *What do witches add to childhood?*

For renewal open the door to the irrational.

19 Fear

Image: *The mouse's tail sticks out of its hole.*

'Only the ego feels fear.'

So you are afraid? You don't know what to do and perhaps want to run, to hide, to feel safe. Safe from what? From the Great Adversary? From life itself? There are so many things to be afraid of in this life. Life is so hard, so full of suffering and difficulties.

Yet why fear anything at all? All that is out there is life itself, life to be lived to the fullest, life which includes the good and the bad, the creative and the destructive. Life, I love every part of it, its danger and destructiveness as well as its warmth and happiness. May we all be given life in equal measure, the great opposites themselves.

But none of us start out that way. Do we? Are children more open to life as it is than adults? Certainly open children live more fully than closed adults. Life is for living. Therefore, I am for all of it. Give me the whole thing or I will not do well with any of it.

Some of us are still rejecting certain parts of life as stupid, evil, awful, and so on. Those with the greatest fears seem to do the most rejecting of life. Where I fear there also I reject, and in rejecting I am missing important aspects of life.

Only the ego feels fear. And what is fear? When I perceive the possibility of my own annihilation, I feel fear. I am afraid when I perceive I may lose something, even my life. When I feel fear it may be important to take measures to protect myself, or others, or things which I deem valuable. But at times to be identified with anything in this life, even one's own soul or body, can cause us to withdraw fearfully into ourselves and avoid the adversarial aspects of existence.

What we identify with is what we most fear to lose. Adversity is that which opposes. Some event or force comes into our lives and loosens us from whatever we are identified with. Our health, our money, our job, relationships, a way of behaving, values, needs. If at these times of challenge I contract in fear, trying to hold on desperately, I will not have the flexibility to make the necessary shifts in consciousness to better deal with the situation. Rather than contract in fear, open in the fact of challenge, go through the fires of your own transformation and make the necessary shifts to cope with a changing reality. Fear lights the way to possible danger but must never itself be allowed to be the danger.

What was I as a child afraid of? Falling down and hurting myself? Losing my parents? Being rejected by others? Having things I held dear stolen from me? Getting attacked and bullied? The list is endless. Did everything I fear happen to me? Yes! Obviously, being afraid does not stop the adversary from regularly entering my life.

It is not what goes wrong in life which is to be feared, but fear itself. Fear is that which can contract us and force us to choose retreat and inadequacy. If you want to be with that man or woman, go after them. You may fail. You failed many times in childhood and still made it, maybe barely, into adult life. You will fail, and you will succeed, but only by leaping the barrier of imagined inadequacy. Life is what comes your way when you actively choose it.

The Work

- *What were the things you were most afraid of in childhood? How did you deal with each of them? How do they connect with what you are afraid of now? What are your successes in dealing with fear and its inhibiting, anti-life quality.*

- *Describe your fear pattern and how you can bring choice to what you go through.*

We fear what we most need.

20 Playing the Power Game

Image: *Children riding up and down on a see-saw.*

'The frail little bouncy baby must assert its power.'

What we are most afraid of is our own annihilation. Somewhere back in youth our parents, siblings or society tried to win the power-struggle. They sought to dominate and make us do what they wanted. They used power to physically, or verbally, abuse us. Poking at children, calling them names, hitting them, invading them, teasing them, are all attempts to act strong by making the other person weak.

Thus the source of child abuse is the perpetrator's own feelings of inadequacy. Most parents practise child abuse to a certain degree. Anyone who invades another's life is at the edge of abusing them. Parents who ask their children countless questions may be abusing their children by making them 'tell all.' Other parents come into their children's rooms whenever they want, or read their mail, listen to their phone conversations, read their journals. These 'milder' examples still illustrate the invasiveness of parents who often assume that they have a right to know and inspect their children's inner lives. The effect of such behaviour on children is to weaken their sense of boundaries and self-identity and to make them withdraw or fight back in sometimes secret and manipulative ways.

Because children are smaller and dependent for shelter, sustenance and caring, they must compromise with the environment in which they are forced to live. Immediately they find that others are not always there to meet their needs. All babies cry when they are in pain. Their suffering usually causes the adults to act, to hold them, to feed them, to give them love. This is the baby asserting its own power, for it knows instinctively that it is already in competition for the attention of the adults. The frail little bouncy baby must assert its power. But some adults do not respond, turn off, leave the baby alone in its cradle despite its screaming, or even hit it to shut it up. Most parents have had these thoughts, and some act on them. The insecure adult may start trying to win the power game, may try to dominate the baby in its struggle to have its needs met. In repressing the child the adult is repressing his or her own wounded, inner child. How sad!

Somewhere in childhood those with power might have defeated

you, drove you into yourself where you hid. They won the power game. They did not practise the great and valuable principle of 'balance the power, do not try to defeat it.' Meet the child's needs, but in a way that you can meet some of your own needs as well. Let the child win sometimes. Let the child develop into a strong individual by encouraging self-assertion. Only come in and oppose where safety and strong values are at risk.

In the adult years if you act out the childhood manipulation pattern you developed to get your needs met in a family where parents practised a power struggle, you will be defeating yourself. You can learn to ask for what you need in order to get your needs met directly. You can be with people who do not try to win the power game over you. And you can recognise when you attempt to force your way through others' needs in an attempt to meet your own.

Being overwhelmed by someone playing the power game against you can also be perceived as fear. Learn to cope with fear by taking action. You can seize the initiative and stand up for yourself. Develop your own power and balance energy with anyone else who comes your way. You can do it. You can begin to do it now by acting with directness and using the power available to you.

The Work

- *What are your attitudes towards power? What childhood experiences helped create them?*

- *What was your earliest experience of being overwhelmed, or almost overwhelmed, by someone else's power? What defences or manipulation patterns did you develop out of that? Are they in effect today? If so, how can you transform them?*

- *In a meditative state, go back to an early childhood trauma of being defeated in a power struggle and this time keep asserting yourself, equalising somehow the other's force. See what finally happens. You will be changing a pattern inside.*

- *In the next month be aware of situations in which you lost your power to another out of fear. Rehearse what you could have done differently, and keep rehearsing until you have built a habit of asserting yourself in a sometimes adversarial world.*

- *Practice balancing the power in every situation and see what it evokes for you. Trace feelings and attitudes back to childhood*

55

where appropriate. Create new attitudes and self-images of
someone who is usually able to balance power with power.

The twin measures of power are meaning and effectiveness.

21 Rejection

Image: *A refrigerator door found washed up on the sand.*

'No one can reject us but ourselves.'

Everyone seems to have a rejection problem, from the most traumatised to the most supported in childhood. Rejection is then a problem for the ego to deal with, a problem inherent to the ego's dynamics.

No one can reject us but ourselves. Yet we go around afraid of the Big No, afraid that someone will reject us. People can say 'no' to us a million times in this life, but no one can reject us unless we reject ourselves.

Unless we negate ourselves, we cannot be negated by others. So why this fear, this apprehension that I will not get what I want or need? If we identify with a negation we will be subsumed under its power. If I am afraid of the 'no's' in life, I will not risk trying to get to the 'yes.' To not risk experiencing the fullest possibilities in life is 'The Great Negation.'

Why wait for the best to be handed to you without any intention or effort on your part? Chances are you will wait forever. What I need is what I ask for. What I ask for generates what I am likely to get. What I get, no matter how unexpected or contrary, is what I need, and what I need in life is to affirm its fullest potential.

Go back to childhood again and experience there your first great rejection. So what! It was time for your next lesson in the game of life. But did you learn it? Or are you still depriving yourself in the way others deprived you? We reject ourselves because others have rejected us.

And today? Today I will begin a total programme. Today I will not reject myself by saying 'no' to my desires before anyone can say 'no' to me. If you can take 'no' for an answer, you can ask for anything.

The Work

- *List some ways you still cannot take 'no' for an answer. What is the pattern or gut feeling underlying it all? How well do you say 'no' to other people? If you have a problem saying 'no', list*

*some possible attitudes and feelings which may be behind this
inability.*

- *How is not saying 'no' to others actually saying 'no' to
  yourself? Did you think that you could escape saying 'no' in
  life?*

- *List some things you will ask for in the coming week, and list
  after each one, how many 'no's you will accept before you
  give up trying to get what you want.*

- *What is the biggest 'NO' you are afraid of? How might you
  reduce it in size? What was the 'no' your parents gave you?
  What 'no' would it have been good for your parents to have
  given you?*

- *Write up an early childhood experience of rejection. Write the
  attitudes embedded in your description. Write up the effect of
  this experience and resulting attitudes on your behaviour
  today.*

- *What is your rejection problem? And what is its possible
  transformation?*

- *Visualise your ideal parent accepting you fully. What is the
  interaction? How do you respond?*

We reject the possible for fear of the impossible.

22 Speech

Image: *Leaves falling endlessly from innumerable trees.*

'We talk to hear ourselves.'

No sooner out of the womb, in fact while still in the belly of the mother, the baby cries or gurgles in pleasure. We are born to make sounds, to affect others around us. We are born to convey the measure of our experience. Speech is the second birth.

Unfortunately as we became adults the words and sounds of our mouths become as tired as old branches falling. We do not say what we mean. We complain about life. We talk it out and often go on living the same old way. Our words have lost their integrity, their ability to change us or others. Why?

This is what many of us learned in childhood about speech.

- We learned that words did not matter. It was the actions which counted.

- We learned that we could say only part of what we thought. We had to begin censoring our words, thus causing a split in our personalities between the part we could show to the world and the hidden, often more true, part of ourselves.

- We learned that the adults did not listen to most of what we had to say. The adults did not understand us and were selective about what they wanted to hear.

- We learned that we were to tell the truth, but we saw that the adults lied to each other and described the facts about our own person differently from the way we perceived them.

- We learned that it was safer to lie or not say anything in order to protect ourselves from adult power used to dominate us.

- We learned also that the grown-ups wanted us to say everything which was on our minds but that sometimes they would use that information against us. They would embarrass us in front of our friends, punish us for wrong-doing. We gradually learned to keep our mouths shut with the unfortunate result that we felt alienated from others and even from ourselves.

- We learned that talk was dangerous. You had to learn to say the right thing or you would upset someone. We learned that we could not say what we felt because no one could take it, not the adults and not most of our peers.

So as we grew up to be adults, our speech became degraded. Now we must change that. If we do not express ourselves we will not express life. All words express something essential about life. Although some words seem good and others seem bad, they all have their places as expressions of reality.

Some of us use talk as a verbal masking. We talk non-stop about ourselves, not allowing pauses in the conversation for silence, or for the other person to respond. We are preventing intimacy by controlling the verbal impression the other person receives. As mature people we can learn to heal our tongues. We can learn to say what we mean, give voice to what we feel, listen carefully to others, articulate the language colourfully, and use it to be effective in the world.

Others say little but think much. They are afraid to express who they are and hide behind the mask of silence. They need to learn to put themselves verbally out into the world, to share themselves and to give up alienation and unbonding.

Verbalising is a reflective process to make conscious what is happening to us. First we live the experience, and then we reflect upon it, trying to find the meaning in what we just lived out. Most of us talk our lives through with others. We talk to affirm our life and consciousness, to convey value and experience to others. We listen carefully to make contact with another person, and to change. To fully hear someone is to let their words affect you. If you leave an in-depth conversation unchanged, you have not heard what was being said. Talk, then, is the interweaving of inner content with outer reality, the healing bridge which cures alienation, and which brings the joy of living to the world.

The Work

- *What are some of your earliest memories of speech as a child? What seems to be reflected in these memories about yourself?*

- *What was your childhood talk pattern like, and how is it still in effect today? Use the text above to analyse how you did or didn't talk. How is this pattern still active today, and what can you do about it?*

- *Were you honest as a child? What kind of lying did you do? Where would you lie today? What does lying do for you?*

- *What commitments can you make as to how you use speech for growth and direction in life? Examples might be, to say how you feel no matter the circumstances, or to express what is going on inside you at various times throughout the day.*

- *How did you express yourself today using words? What are some ways you might become more expressive and real in the use of words?*

- *Practise listening to someone else and resaying some of what they say so that you may practise accurately perceiving another person's thoughts and words.*

- *To free up your language for more feeling responses, practise talking in imagery. Open up to your unconscious and let the images come. Also give personal reactions to what you say. This is the feeling response.*

Hear what you say and you will say what you feel.

23 Regression

Image: *The toilet bowl has flooded over.*

'... every regression... is an attempt to return to childhood...'

Oh, I don't want to get out of bed today. I'm so tired and basically lazy. And so it goes on. Sometimes life seems so hard. I'm an adult now. I have responsibilities and an image of maturity to maintain. But what hard work this life is! Leave me alone, will you? I want to regress a little.

The regressive pull is a mighty force in our lives. We have all these goals and things we have to do, but somehow we can't quite get going to do them them. We should be growing and productive all the time, but it never works that way. Two steps forward and one step back, sometimes one step forward and two steps back.

Creative regression is to consciously slip out of our known adult personality, the images of maturity with which we are identified, and slide back a number of years to earlier behaviour. Some of us are so identified with our personas that we find it amazingly difficult to consciously choose moments of creative regression.

'I'm going to rest now, I will let go and have some fun. I'm not going to do anything today, nothing! The whole world can go to hell as far as I am concerned. Let's play and act like little animals. Wouldn't that be fun?'

If we do not consciously regress from time to time in order to escape the adult persona and find renewal, regression will take over when we can least afford it. Sickness will strike when we need to be well. Sleepiness, spacing out, losing things, drinking, forgetting – there is a long list of unconscious regressions we escape into in order to find renewal. But unless these ways of regressing are brought to consciousness, we will remain at war with ourselves.

Creative regression can take us back to that place of the child, the original spontaneity and creative flexibility for life. Take moments throughout the day to just let go of everything, like a two or five minute nap. Allow yourself to be playful and act like a child where appropriate, or nearly appropriate. A momentary laugh may be a letting go.

We are re-experiencing our childhood in order to live it more fully and bring it to completion. One of the results will be that we can more easily let go of our adult persona and find renewal in the inner child. So, in effect, every regression, planned or not, is an attempt to return to childhood and can be dealt with as such. Love the child and let go a little – or a lot!

The Work

- *What are your typical forms of compulsive or unconscious regressing? Describe them and what might evoke them. Define creative alternatives to meet the needs causing these regressions.*

- *In what ways were you too mature when you were young and therefore missed being a child? What aspects of being the child have you not had a chance to live fully? Everything? Pin down what you missed the most. How might your present regression pattern be influenced by this?*

- *List creative ways you might regress a little during your day, to find renewal.*

- *Write a positive statement about yourself which includes your ability to regress. 'I am good at regressing...'*

We lose ourselves to find ourselves.

24 The Family Archetype

Image: *The forest on the mountain burns.*

'Many make the choice to preserve the family at all costs.'

The family archetype, unintegrated, is a motivating force in many of the difficulties of adult life. Most of humankind go to their graves never having become conscious of themselves because they remain in the family archetype.

Examples of the power of the family archetype over adults include the following – living next to one's parents all one's life; calling parents 'mum' and 'dad' in adult life instead of addressing them by their names. Married people calling each other 'Mum' and 'Dad' is another extreme. 'Mum' and 'Dad' are not real people but archetypes, symbolic primaries without individuality.

To graduate into adult life we must break the archetypal hold which inner and outer parents have on us. If we cannot call our parents by their real names, at least some of the time, then we keep ourselves identified with being a child, a form of dependency. We also do not do our part to help challenge 'mum' and 'dad' to become real people in their own eyes and regarding us.

Does one need to give up the family in order to get free of unconscious domination by the archetype? Most of us certainly must liberate ourselves physically and psychologically in a number of ways. But wholehearted rejection of the family is not the solution because no matter how far we run, the childhood family stays inside us until it has been dealt with. In solving the family problem we will become free to better relate to the family as an inner and outer experience. We can become more loving because we have extricated ourselves from the prison of the archetype.

Can we individuate, or follow our path, and achieve inner wholeness within the family?

The forces causing us to play different roles within a family system are so powerful that it may not seem possible both to individuate and put your family first. In childhood you tried to become yourself and look what happened. The family attempted to break and claim you for its own. You needed to resist to find your own being and way.

Yet individuation is possible for a family as well, and its members.

The Primal Family

This would take an open family structure in which all members seek to balance power rather than give it away or grab it, and in which members share and process everything which comes up.

The family image of the future will be one of wholeness, of nesting, fertility and relationship which creates new life, one that creates out of itself the freedom to both journey alone and in the company of those who are our true companions. We may leave the original family behind, but we will find others of like mind and heart with whom to journey and achieve a common purpose in life.

The Work

- *What is your position on calling your parents 'mum' and 'dad'? What do you think their position is? Fantasise what might happen if you told them you wanted to use their adult names in relating to them. If you have the courage, choose to call your parents by their real names and not Mum and Dad. Feel what this does for your inner growth.*

- *In what ways are you still trying to live your childhood family life in your adult primary relationships?*

- *How have you sought the ideal family in certain group experiences? How have you tried to work out your own childhood pattern in groups with authority figures? What failed? What did you learn about yourself and groups?*

Wholeness without is only possible from wholeness within.

25 The Family Dynamics

Image: *The string is full of knots.*

'Family dynamics ... enable strange and different people ... to live together.'

You are back in childhood again. Everything that happened to you has a purpose, some lesson for you to learn. You were born into a web, and you contributed to the configuration of that web whether you knew it or not. You studied and played at how things worked in your family. Who was beholden to whom? Where were the points of power? You studied what you had to fear and what was only bluff, what you could get away with and what was dangerous to do. And you found where the power lay which was yours, yours because for the others in the family your power depended on their secret weaknesses.

Did you become your mother's confidant, able to hear what would not even be told to your father? Were you in league with the old man, knowing how to ride on his hidden feelings? How did you manage to make your corner of the nest secure against the intrusions of brothers and sisters? And what did you do about the family shadow, the ghosts hidden in the closet, the neurosis passed from generation to generation which no one was willing to talk about? Did you choose, in fact, to break free of it so that your children would not suffer the same fate you did? Or do you still not have children of your own for this reason?

Family dynamics are those patterns established unconsciously to enable strange and different people, who call themselves a family, to live together. In order to maintain the pattern, we each give up something essential to our own being, we make the grand sacrifice as our contribution to the sovereignty of the family archetype.

Let us include in the family picture some of the more positive patterns and practices, like singing songs together, which give the family warmth and life. Our goal is consciousness. We want to choose and transform. We want to redeem that lost child who had to adapt at the price of not being able to become her or his unique self. At their best, family dynamics support and make real major potentials as the individuals grow and change through life.

The Work

- A *number of important questions have been raised in the above passage. Which questions did you gravitate towards? Create a full response to one or two, or all if you choose to take the time.*

- *Make a drawing of each of the members of your primary childhood family. After you are finished, write feeling reactions to your picture. Then describe the picture to someone else so that you may make conscious the dynamics in what you drew.*

- *Make a diagram of power in your family. Try to describe the different kinds of power each family member had. What was your kind of power?*

- *Write a description of you in your room, what you did there, and what kind of a refuge it was for you. What were you seeking refuge from? What happened there in your own solitude?*

To find the pattern, find your unique place in the pattern.

26 The Garden of the Heart

Image: *The wind has blown the covers off the bed.*

'Everything had a place and a story.'

Once, long ago, in a wonderful room somewhere lived a little girl, or was it a little boy? And in that room were many magical things which only little people knew about. And this place was known by the spirits which lived there with the little person as 'the garden of the heart.'

In the room was a bed and on the pillow of that bed was a small doll, or was it a stuffed animal? Or was it even a tiny being? It might have been anything in that rainbow room. All we know is that to the person who lived there many things were alive, not least of which were the beings who lay on the pillow every day and night or sat on certain shelves in the room.

And there were books in that room, picture books and word books and old books and new books and books you could smell and books you could get a big person to look at and tell you a story from. And then one day you yourself could open the pages and hear the story inside yourself as your eyes moved across the page.

It was a room in which to be alone. Most of the time the big people would stay out of your place. They had rooms of their own they liked to go to. You could hide from the big ones and see pictures and tell stories. You could bring a friend like yourself into your own space, and he or she would know you through your room and make up stories with you about what went on there which nobody but yourselves knew about.

There was the secret of the bottom drawer, the secret of the tiny man who lived there and one could not see unless one looked very closely, and even then you might miss him or be in danger of sniffing him up into your nose. You half suspected that you had sniffed up many little beings in your room because from time to time you had to sneeze and never knew why. You learned to aim towards the bottom drawer which you always kept open a crack just in case, and your mother never understood any of this and was always tidying up and closing the drawer on you.

Oh, there were so many things alive in the garden of your heart as you lived among your real people as you called them. Everything had a place and a story. Many beings talked to you and you hoped you were a good listener, and you always acted on what they had to say, and had to ask their permission before you could fall asleep at night.

And now so many miles and years away from that room it all seems gone from you, an image out of the past never to be lived again. Can you see it floating away down to your left? Those rooms and companions you had in the old days seem to have faded, and in their place is the painting on the wall, the crack in the ceiling, the photograph on your desk, the clothes in the closet. When you are gone the ones that survive you will come in and sort everything out. Some leftovers they will put in boxes, some will be thrown out or given away. But how will anyone ever know that secret world, the child's room and the adult's living space, how will they ever know what inhabited the garden of your heart?

The Work

- *What did your childhood room mean to you as a child? Write about it and how it served as a focus for your life. What was your parents' relationship to your room? What inside yourself represents your childhood room?*

- *Take a favourite object, a doll, stuffed animal perhaps, then describe it or have an active imagination dialogue with it. Ask it to give you a description of what you were like as a kid. How does this affect you now as an adult?*

A true secret never survives the telling of it.

27 The Wondrous Child

Image: *The cocoon is laced with gold which the child holds.*

'Find this lost child and you will find life.'

This child exists somewhere, inside us. Perhaps we embodied him way back there in the beginnings of our childhood, perhaps we will see him personified in the physical child we will bring into the world. Or we may only know the existence of this child by a near-silent ache somewhere. Most likely you have seen the child, when you saw someone's child do something which was absolutely right for that moment. For an instant, you felt what it could be like to be the child of life. It was your own inner child who gave you a glimpse of the radiance.

At the darkest time of year, the Winter Solstice, we celebrate in this culture the birth of the Divine Child, another term for experiencing the Wondrous Child within us. At Christmas people act with a little more wonder, more caring, more joy, more giving. The Gift, the archetypal symbol of life, is offered from the heart. For what is the great gift each of us receives if not life itself? What we do with this gift is our choice. At the darkest time of the year we make sacred the birth of the new light. Thus each year we seek renewal through contact again with the Wondrous Child archetype, that dynamic which represents new spiritual birth in our lives.

Unfortunately, also at the Christmas season many are afflicted with sadness and even acute despair. At that time the wounded child comes up instead of the wondrous child. People who cannot return home to family and childhood feel left out, lonely, on the edge of depression. And even within the regular families all is not always well. There is bickering, manipulation and outright fighting, as the wounded child pops out trying to be recognised where the wondrous child is supposed to reign supreme.

The truth is that many parents unconsciously or consciously hurt or kill our wondrous side as children. We became identified with the wounded child and the wondrous child disappeared or hid in the world of fantasy. We entered adulthood repressed and too serious, and therefore unable to express wonder and joy on a daily level. We lost our sense of creativity, the mystery, the flexibility to grow and

71

change, no matter what the circumstance. For the wondrous child represents in us that spontaneous creative dynamic which can respond to any situation with openness and freshness. As adults, if we enter a growth process we have a chance to face our wounded child and resurrect our wondrous child. We revive the happy child in us to get out of a repressed and compulsive childishness which refuses to let us become fully involved in life. We welcome the wondrous child in the joy which comes through conscious fulfilment of much that we are meant to be.

The Work

- *Write a flowing description of your wondrous child. What was he or she like?*

- *At what point did that wondrous child get lost? What was the trauma? What defence system had to be built to protect what was left of you?*

- *Have a dialogue with your wondrous child. Ask what or how this child can come alive in you now.*

- *Recall some of your most vivid memories of experiencing children as truly alive and expressing a certain essence. What qualities for you are being expressed in these experiences.*

- *Write a description of an integrated family experience of Christmas, Hanukkah, Winter Solstice or New Year.*

The joy of being creates the radiance to love.

28 The Body

Image: *In two hands is cupped living earth.*

'Truly the body is the vessel of love, not hate.'

When we think of the body of the very small child, we think of vulnerability and nappies, of smiles and cries, of perfection and miracle, of smooth warm skin, suckling and eating pleasure, and of all the amazing growth and pushing through of form which seems to take place daily. The body is perfect in itself in all its functions. Then why as adults do we hide and chastise certain bodily functions so?

Parents quickly enough socialise their new born and growing infants. Clean up the faeces and urine. It takes time but we are taught to control our bowels and our sexuality. The urges of the body do not necessarily get met when the urge is there. Do not teach the child by right and wrong or by disgust. Teach the child to be aware of the animal sides of himself and learn to be appropriate so as not to cause unnecessary anguish. But as you teach the small child, do not condemn him for being the animal he is. And as an adult have mercy on your own animal, the body which is you, which is life, which lives, grows, expresses energy, has wastes and dies.

The ego tends to identify with the body. My body is me. Yet who am I? I do not always feel in my body. Sometimes I may go for hours in some activity without realising that I am in a body. Then I feel the physical strain, the urge to eat and defecate and I remember where I am.

And where am I? Was I taught in my early body-control training to see myself negatively? If my faeces or sexuality disgust me then I am less likely to see myself in a positive light. I produce that stuff which is hard for others. I am the menses, the urine, the semen and the excrement. So there. I am a creator at all times. To live I must take in and give out. Do you then accept me? Do I then accept myself?

In sickness and in health. Was it hard in childhood to be sick, to feel that which was me, vulnerable and painful? Was I nurtured enough when sick? Or did I learn that to be sick was a hassle and that people only liked me when I was well? Or I only get attention when I am ill?

Return to the body. The great message for today's world is, 'Who is truly alive and accepting their bodies? Would anyone kill another body in war and murder who knew the value of being alive in the body?'

Truly the body is the vessel of love, not hate.

The Work

- *What are your feelings about defecating? Write them out. Heal them by seeing yourself 'taking a dump' as a kid and having a good time with it.*

- *What rituals do you have when 'going to the bathroom.' What is the control pattern involved? Or the releasing pattern?*

- *And now for your genitals. What were some early frightening experiences to do with your genitals? What did you do? What was your pattern? What was your parents' response? Now for healing, see yourself as a child playing and having fun with your genitals. What is the value of your experience?*

- *Expressing sexuality or bodily waste involves our holding and releasing patterns. What is yours? Write it out fully. Then see where you can make some changes. Deal with the anxiety which results from this. It is new energy for life being released. Create with it.*

What we love will love us.

29 Guilt

Image: *A dark-coned tornado.*

'For guilt, substitute acceptance.'

Guilt, an oppressive word, positive to a few, but to a great many of us an agonising experience of inhibiting the life force. Most of us say we feel guilty, but what is it that we feel? Perhaps what we feel is tension, some conflict of opposing views and forces tearing us apart.

Guilt is the tension I feel between trying to meet my needs and living up to my own or someone else's expectations.

In childhood the parents might have said that we should be kind to our playmates, and if we were not kind then we were bad children. But a child does not always feel kindness. A child may want to meet his or her own needs for possessing things or expressing anger and aggression. The child experiences a tension between meeting his own needs and conforming to adult expectations. And if the child follows his own way, he risks being judged as a bad child. Hence Guilt.

'I am bad because I put myself first before others.'

Why feel bad because you did not fulfil someone else's need? And why make others feel wrong when they do not meet your needs?

To free ourselves from guilt, we must take the risk of expressing and pursuing our own needs and let others fulfil their own wants and desires. When needs clash, negotiate and compromise. In place of judging put actions and their consequences. It is not wrong for me to try and meet my needs first. It may be upsetting, and that is what I must deal with.

Whole systems of ethics and morality have been created to make us feel bad. If we go against the thousand and one commandments then we are judged a bad person. If we conform to collective values then we get rewarded by receiving approval and having our needs honoured by the collective's power. To conform we must live in fear of doing the wrong thing and being disapproved of for doing it.

A creative way of dealing with needs is to encourage each person to express his or her own needs, and to work together for everyone's fulfilment. In order to do this we must give up judgement and blaming. We are not bad people nor do we need to make anyone else a bad person. For guilt, substitute acceptance, embrace the differences, find common ground. We are the stuff that dreams are made of!

The Work

- *List the things or situations which seem to create the most guilt for you. How would this be a good description of your shadow, that side of you which is the repository of what you have rejected and otherwise hidden away because it was somehow unacceptable, or guilt producing?*

- *Write up how you were punished as a child. What guilt, what fear, did this cause in you, and what were the attitudes towards yourself and life resulting from this? As an adult how do you deal or not deal with the consequences of your choices?*

- *Try meeting only your needs for a day. Consistently tell other people 'no' and at the same time deal with the tension which this produces. What attitudes underlie the tension you are experiencing? Then try only meeting other people's needs for a day. What shifts in attitude and consciousness seem to result?*

- *Finally, practise balance in each situation. Always get a need met at the same time you are meeting someone else's need. If yours and the other person's needs cannot both be met, stay in the creative tension until you find a way through to something new.*

Feel and you will not pass judgement.

30 Play

Image: *The tumbleweed blows across the prairie.*

'To play the game of life is to not be identified with it.'

We play when we act but do not identify with the action. Work is when we are identified with what we do.

The child plays at doctor, accident, war, house, making babies. The child copies the adults and rehearses the adult life by playing it out. The adult, on the other hand, takes Work as real by identifying with it, and to identify with anything is to be caught in it. To play the game of life is to not be identified with it. When we are not identified with what we do we have more flexibility and creativity available. If you do not like doing something, or cannot get into it because you cannot see yourself as it, then play with the energy, try it out as just a game.

Adults are identified with being adult. Children, on the other hand, are not as identified with being children. They play at all the roles of life. The adult gets lazy, picks a small number of roles and tries to identify with these, causing many deaths in the personality. To identify with one thing is to reject other things. 'I am a good person' means 'I am not a bad person.' In actuality, being human, we are both.

We can return to play, not competition, not winning and losing, but dancing into and out of an experience with a sense of discovery and endless possibility. We play to get out of our known selves. Branch out. Be everybody. To laugh is to recognise that we have over-identified with ourselves. To laugh and play, to express the child in us, is the renewal by which we are born anew each day.

The Work

- *What would you do if you made a decision to play at least once a day?*

- *What are the three things in yourself or in life with which you are most identified? What causes you to be identified with them?*

- *What in terms of play might help you become free of your identifications?*

- *In what ways were you too serious as a child?*

- *In what ways did you let yourself play as a child? Why these areas and not others?*

- *What would be your own definition of play?*

- *Design a play programme for yourself. Or take your main activities and add a play element to them.*

Play kindles the flames of renewal and letting go.

31　The First Choice

Image: *A hidden waterfall under a mountain.*

'At the end of that long train ride into my future I made someone pay a little for my suffering.'

My earliest memory of making a choice was at the age of six when I was sent off to boarding school, never again to live in my parents' home. I can see it now, the little boy dressed up with the name tag hanging around his neck. My mother is telling me about courage. My father is carrying my suitcase. In my heart I don't know why this is happening. I cannot comprehend the inevitable. Yet it is happening to me. I want to cry, but I am supposed to be strong. I want to cling, but I am supposed to be independent. I want to stay at home, but I am forced to take a journey.

I was placed on the train leaving New York City's Grand Central Station and given the name of the town in upper New York state where I was to get off and be met by the school staff. I was to listen for the conductor's calling out each station as we came to it. The conductor was also to make sure I got off at the right station. The conductor called out 'Hope Farm'. I knew this was my destination, but in my child's mind I was not sure. I was not absolutely certain that I had heard right. I wanted to do the right thing so I waited. The train moved on again. I think I went to the conductor and the school people had to drive to the next town and pick me up for my new life.

It seemed I had no choice in the matter. I had to leave home at age six. I just had to leave. That's all. Destiny was handing me an uncommon blow, and what would I do with it?

What choices did I have? Perhaps even in this forced situation I still had choice. There is always a measure of freedom given to us in any moment. How well do we take and use that freedom?

At the end of that long train ride into my future I made someone pay a little for my suffering. But I also weakened my choice-making ability by my hesitation and insecurity. I could have gone with what I knew was right, that this was my station and I had to accept the change fully. If I got off at the wrong station and there was no one there to meet me, it would be like stepping off into the void. I would leave my new home, the train, and step out into nothingness. It was so hard at that moment to trust in the future and in strangers.

The early choices are the crucial, the mythic ones. To this day, I can become extremely anxious when faced with preparing for a trip. But the pattern is changing. Strong choice becomes the necessity and the cure. Choice is directing energy in one direction and not another. Automatic actions are not choices in this sense. To choose we must place ourselves within the tension of mutually exclusive alternatives. Saying 'Yes' to one thing is saying 'No' to all which would oppose it.

I was given destiny at an early age. I was awakened from childhood. I was given a rough choice. I was to bear the consequences of someone else's cruel choice. Yet within the context of it all I still had some freedom, and it is upon that which I evaluate my behaviour. Perhaps, in staying on the train I made the choice I was capable of. I could think of nothing else. It has taken years to work through the insecurity which has plagued my choice-making ability. And now I love my myth. For I was given, in the black light of consciousness, the power of choice. Nothing is certain in this world except our necessity to make choices.

The Work

- *Was what happened to me in childhood fair in your estimation? What do you mean by fairness? How does justice relate to choice-making?*

- *What is your earliest or most significant childhood memory of choice-making on your part? Be specific and write about it. Let the feelings and imagery come up. Then analyse your choice-making, or lack of choice-making, pattern.*

- *Describe how you make choices. On what basis do you usually make choices? Feelings? Others' opinions? Intuition? Thinking rationally about the situation? Doing what is right according to your beliefs? Other?*

What we choose is what we become.

32 The Journey

Image: *A wooden staff carved by the The Maker.*

'The great question is, are we fulfilling ourselves at the deepest of levels?'

'Once upon a time ... and they lived happily ever after.' Yes, but what is between the beginning and the end of every folk tale? The Journey.

'Once upon a time ...' starts us out in eternal time back at the beginning of things, and is the prelude for our entering the Now of the story. And '...they lived happily ever after' takes us back into eternity. Life may be seen as a journey when we recognise that what we are going through has underlying universal patterns for realising the meaning of life. The archetypes are the primaries of existence and every journey contains those primaries within it. It is our fate to encounter crisis as Death-Rebirth, sexuality as the striving for unity in the Self, a continual movement forward in life as the Journey, sickness as the Adversary, prosperity and new life as the Heroic, caring as the Feminine, and structuring as the Masculine. Do we resist any of these archetypes? Then we resist the Journey and seek refuge in unconsciousness.

How each of the primary elements play themselves out in each person's life will differ, even among twins. Perhaps in childhood you had a huge dose of the Adversary and needed to almost overdevelop its opposite, the Heroic? Or perhaps, in striving for the unity you did not have, you seek much sexual activity? Whatever the dynamics, we can make them conscious and create balance and resolution in our lives.

Each person has a destiny to realise in this life. The question is, are we fulfilling ourselves at the deepest of levels? To do this we must accept fully whatever comes our way, in sickness and in health, in good fortune and in bad, and in dealing with all the contraries which are our lot.

It all started back in childhood. What was the journey for us then? What did we resist and what did we accept? We return now to those experiences in childhood to make them conscious and integrate the totality of what happened to us. We see and re-experience the Journey as it carried us through childhood. The Journey continues into adult life and finally to the end of all our days.

Some Sayings for the Journey

We are already the goal of what we would become.

To journey is to go where you hesitate to go.

To journey is to know right where you are.

There is no going back. The return takes us to the end of all our days.

You will only know where you are going when you get there.

What we least expect is what happens to us.

Never look back or you will be blind to the future.

To journey is to match inner life to outer.

We spend the first half of life catching up, and the second half moving ahead.

Live the process and the goals will take care of themselves.

The goal of life is what you do now, not later.

There is no future, only your becoming in the now.

A riderless horse never seeks a master.

Moving towards sunset may bring the sunrise.

There is no return, only completion.

You are already on a journey. The task is to find what journey you are on.

The Work

- *Construct a journey map of the first six years of childhood, including your roots going back before you were born. Include experiences related to the various topics we have been dealing with. To create a journey map you draw a winding road on successive sheets of paper linked together. Include intersections and other roads leading into and going away from it. You also label and draw little figures and scenes representing your primary experiences. Primaries might include you as journeyer, parents, other family members, crucial or strong events, traumas, gifts' spiritual experiences. The list is endless. You might make a cut-out of you as journeyer, and cut-outs for anyone or anything which goes with you. Don't forget your mythic experiences and figures.*

- *In what ways are you on and not on a journey? Have you committed yourself to following the path of greatest meaning in life? Or have you focused on worldly and collective goals and values as substitutes for the Journey? To journey is to move below the surface of things. We don't all make it.*

- *Write up your first six years and before as a folk tale using the traditional motifs. 'Once upon a time so-and-so lived in a...., and had to deal with...., and was helped by...., and was almost overwhelmed by...., and finally got to...., and lived harmoniously until the next gate opened in her, or his, journey.' There are other motifs and aspects of a typical folk tale, of course. Create what works for you. Perhaps read again your favourite folk tale and then go from there. Let it flow!*

Life puts you on the road but how you walk it is your affair.

33 Which Sex Were Each of Your Parents?

Image: *Crossed sticks in the middle of the path.*

'My father mothered me and my mother told me what to do. Am I confused?'

The great, well-kept secret is that our parents often changed 'sexes' right before our eyes. No wonder we became confused and unclear about which role models to follow. Am I a boy, or am I not? Am I a girl or not?

One kind of mother problem can be defined as having grown up in conflict with one's mother's animus, her inner masculine. Did your mother act out her feminine, her caring, accepting and nurturing side? Or was she critical, directing and dominating? One father problem can be having grown up in conflict with one's father's anima, his inner feminine. Was your father strong, definite and structuring? Or was he touchy, passive, and withdrawing? Perhaps some of these characteristics apply to your parental experience in those early years. Our thesis is that often the parent acts out the opposite archetype to the biological predisposition with confusing results.

If I as a boy am seeking nurturing and acceptance from my mother and instead get criticism and domination, I am missing what I feel I need. In this example, my mother is acting from her negative animus. Her animus is out to defeat and destroy my young masculine to keep me chained. And my father's masculine is not strong enough to balance my mother's masculine, so she rules the roost. If however, my mother is able to also act from her feminine and be nurturing and inspiring, then my own masculine can grow and achieve in the world. I will not be in competition with my mother's animus and therefore free to develop.

In my life mother did rule the household. It was she who taught me about great literature and music, who discussed the extraordinary ideas and movements of this century while my father cooked the meals for us, took me to movies and to buy toy guns which I loved. My father was the well known poetry anthologist of the sixties, Oscar Williams, but he never once discussed a serious idea with me. Where was his masculine in relation to his son? I don't know.

Certainly, we each have the opposites within us, but when we express the opposite of our natural dominant in an unconscious and compulsive way we create a loaded atmosphere. How clear are you on your relationship to the archetypes of the Feminine and Masculine? To find out, see how they operated in your parents, and your reactions to what was or was not being expressed. Then make choices to evoke healing energies for balance and integration.

My father mothered me and my mother told me what to do. Am I confused? At least I got something from them. No wonder I wondered who my real parents were!

The Work

- *How did your father act as a mother, and your mother as a father? Or was there some other combination with them? What effect did this have on you?*

- *Did either of your parents want you to be a different sex? If so, what effect has this had on you in terms of masculine and feminine?*

- *How, as a small child, did you evoke your parents' archetypal opposites?*

- *How did you become either a parent's 'symbolic lover', intimate friend, or adversary? How does this pattern affect present intimate relationships?*

What we lack outside can be fulfilled within.

34 The Wounded Child

Image: *The meteorite has fallen out of the sky.*

'Experiencing our wounds can make us whole.'

Who wants to go back into that painful past and experience the worst again? Who wants to experience one's own wounded child? Was she teased unmercifully or violated in some way? Was he punished arbitrarily for things he didn't understand? Did the child feel powerless and therefore act in ways which would upset the parents? Breaking things? Getting into accidents and being hurt? Temper tantrums? Or did one have to be the good child all the time when it would have been so nice to fall apart and be taken care of? But who would have helped us if we had let go to our vulnerability?

Picture the modern scene. We are all clients in therapy with someone. Do we let go there? Do we show our most vulnerable side? Do we trust that the therapist will respond in an accepting and healing way? Perhaps we have tried to let go, to become vulnerable in our intimate, adult relationships, and the other person could not or would not handle this? If someone else cannot handle our vulnerable side, how can we?

Is it so bad to have a wounded child? We hurt. We cry out in pain. We want to avoid painful situations in the present life because they also evoke the unbearable repressed trauma of childhood. Yet we need to work through the wounded child in order to be able to fully deal with the pain natural to adult life. The solution is to let go to vulnerability with one part of oneself while maintaining support and balance with the ego and the Self, the integrative centre. We can seek and receive help from others, but ultimately we must face our own wounded child on our own terms and with our own resources.

It's all right to have a wounded child who breaks out every once in a while. Perhaps it happens in sickness or when we are denied something we think we need. Perhaps the woundedness comes through when we let go in other ways, such as in making love. Or does the wounded child make its presence felt in some nameless anxiety or consuming compulsion, such as greedy over-eating?

The principle is to know and safely express one's wounded child in ways which seem appropriate. Otherwise, this childishness will break out in inappropriate ways, giving us much trouble in order to get our attention. The wounded child is our vulnerability. Experiencing our wounds can make us whole. When we are most vulnerable we are most human, and therefore able to be cared for by ourselves and others. When we are vulnerable we are less arrogant, and therefore easier to approach and be intimate with on a human level. Our vulnerabilty makes us real.

The Work

- *Describe your earliest experience of being wounded.*

- *How would you describe your wounded child? Write in free flowing words and images.*

- *Have a dialogue with your wounded child, how it affects your life right now, and what it wants from you? Then take action.*

- *What is an example of how your wounded child breaks out in adult life? What feelings or issues are usually behind its breaking out?*

- *Finish this sentence, 'I like being vulnerable because...'*

Relationship is shared vulnerability.

35 Childhood's Stories

Image: *Her face has aged a hundred years.*

'I do not know any babies who are fatalistic. I know many adults who are.'

Rock-a-bye baby on the tree top.
When the wind blows the cradle will rock.
When the bough breaks the cradle will fall.
Down will come baby, cradle and all.

Now what kind of a song is this to sing to a baby? This lullaby gives an interesting yet pessimistic viewpoint on life. The fall from grace? The weakness of the support system? Be careful of high places? Do not reach for the sky, little one, or great will be your fall! Life is full of danger, my little one, my baby, and you may not make it. Do not set your sights too high. Expect the worst. And what is baby doing up in that tree in the first place? Is this an unconscious death wish by the parent to be freed of the child and young again? Where is the parent who will protect the baby?

Jack and Jill went up the hill
To fetch a pail of water.
Jack fell down and broke his crown
And Jill came tumbling after.

Dear Jack and Jill,
I want you to know that water is one of the wonderful things in life, and I am glad that you are doing your part in going and getting some water for yourself and others. Sometimes we do take a tumble when we try and help ourselves or others. But much of the time we can walk happily down hills and not fall and break our crowns. And, Jill and Jack, if we can stop war and reduce the level of violence in this world things will go better for you and all of us. Life does not need to be an endless tragedy, and we do not have to feel so helpless when we seek to get our needs met. When you go up that hill to fetch your water, come back down to us also with love and caring in your buckets. Watch your step please. Together we may just make it into a new and better world. I love you. You are doing fine.

Jack and Jill came off the hill
With many pails of water.

88

Jack went down and into town
And Jill came sailing after.

Each one of us in childhood has been drawn to some folk tale or
Mother Goose rhyme. Why a particular one? Looking closely at the
tale or rhyme we can see mirrored there a certain view of the world
which probably has coloured how we see and interact with life as
adults. For transformation sometimes we must go back to the
beginning, to the early lore reflected in images before adult thinking.
The archetypes, the primal energies, are most raw in childhood and in
mental illness. In some ways Mother Goose may reflect a collective
psychosis or archetypal possession from ancient times, and out of
which we are, hopefully, slowly emerging.

I do not know any babies who are fatalistic. I know many adults
who are. For transformation we return to the wondrous child before
the wounded child showed its being.

Yes, there were also the miracle stories, the fairy godmother who
saves Cinderella and helps her out in the end. But I prefer that we not
wait to the end of things for redemption. Wherever there is darkness
and evil, there is also the possibility for its redemption. The child
itself is its own redeemer. Redemption comes in the process of living
life. Redemption, to have major effect, must come in the middle of a
life story, not at the end.

The Work

* *What story or rhyme out of childhood were you most drawn
  to? Look at it closely as you would a dream. How has its
  message influenced your life? Outline the major points of your
  childhood which seem mythic. Then put them into a Mother
  Goose rhyme or into folk tale form. What does this
  experience inspire in you?*

As you believe, so shall you act.

36 The Companion

Image: *A pair of eyes gleam in the night.*

'...we need others in order to find ourselves.'

Life is a lonely business at times, and perhaps always. Ultimately, we are alone in this life. We make connections, some deep and lasting. Yet even before we are on our death bed, we know it, we sense that it's only us in the universe. There are some things we will never be able to share with anyone.

Hence the companion, that mythic journeyer who goes with us down the path of life and even to the edge of eternity. And who is my companion, ultimately? Who is it who understands and brings out that which is essentially me?

Shall I make you my companion this year? Are you the one with whom I can share? Are we soul-mates? Do we have a deep attunement without doing anything to make it happen?

In childhood, many of us had imaginary companions, 'the elementals' as some people would call them. Perhaps they were most present when we were alone, and the adults knew nothing about them? But they talked to the childhood us, and made little magical things happen in our lives. They knew who we were and how we felt. We could tell them anything and they would understand. They had secret powers which they might loan to deal with the crazy life we found ourselves in. Perhaps we saw them as guides, ones who knew the future and made the right things happen, the ones who came to us in our time alone.

Then there was also the best friend, the real outer life friend with whom we did everything and said everything. Well, almost. Sometimes there would be disappointments, conflicts, fights, and we would feel all alone again. Perhaps we wanted our friend to be someone they weren't? But we needed that person to talk to, to move with through our day.

And so comes the point of integration, the realisation that we need others in order to find ourselves. The secret of relationship becomes one of not holding on to the people we relate to, but rather integrating into ourselves the energy they carry and awake in us. We learn that we use our closest intimates to find more of ourselves. I will

90

be a mirror and a companion to you as we live our lives. But in the same way I rely on you to reflect me back to myself so that I may truly become the person I am meant to be. I seek to become a companion to myself, to all of you out there, to life, to my guides, and ultimately the Source which directs me and to which I return at the earthly end.

The Work

- *Describe your imaginary companions in childhood, especially those first years. If you have no factual memory, then meditate and sink back into early childhood, and see yourself with an imaginary companion.*

- *How would you characterise your strongest childhood friendships? What needs were being met or not being met in these relationships?*

- *What are you seeking in companionship these days? What light might the thoughts expressed in the above passage throw on your companionship needs?*

- *What kind of companion are you to others? Evaluate. Where would you like to give more? Where are you giving too much?*

- *What function does your journal play in meeting your needs for companionship? Are you making your children your companions? If so, why? What is wrong with adults?*

We relate to others to relate to ourselves.

37 Playing Victim

Image: *He looks at his hand while it burns.*

'In the family some dominate and some play victim.'

As a child I was terrorised, sexually abused, deprived, spit upon, rejected time and time again. Am I complaining? Do I hate my childhood? Not at all! I realise now that was just good training for playing the victim in life. I didn't go so far as to put my head in the way of a fist during a fight, as another boy did, but I had my tricks. There are two ways to win a fight. One is to overpower and victimise your opponent. The other is to make yourself into the perfect victim. I was never good at the latter, though I could whine and sulk on occasion. I learned to control my tears, to become cold and somewhat hard. I hated the weak, the vulnerable, the crazy, the morally decrepit. I would be the little hero no matter what. But I was a victim at heart.

Playing victim is sinking into despair and lack of direction when reality seems to be presenting me with things other than what I want. When reality becomes my adversary I can play victim by giving up, as if saying, 'all right, if you don't want me to succeed, I won't.'

'What does it matter if things don't go my way? We lose some, we win some. The law of opposites holds sway over our lives. The great archetypal figure of Fortuna, the medieval goddess of fortune who holds the balance scales, will have her way no matter what I choose!'

Wait! These are attitudes. What a thing to tell oneself! Better to say that I am open to any opposite but my choice goes with that which is most unifying and integrating. I may not get what I want, but I will use whatever potentials are present in the situation for the best.

Playing victim is telling oneself that something bad is going to happen anyway, so why try? Playing hero is telling oneself that all is going to turn out to be wonderful, just the way one intends to. Playing victim leads to despair. Playing hero leads to inflation. Surely there is an integrative way.

Playing victim is also a manipulation pattern established in early childhood to get our needs met. The formula is, if we are wounded and helpless someone will take care of us. In the family some dominate and some act the victim. The dominators project their wounded side onto natural victims, they are drawn both to helping and victimising further. The victims project their strong side out onto natural dominators and so stay in dependency. To get free you must give up manipulating with helplessness and take on your own self-healing. Use others for support but more and more do your own work yourself. Wholeness means integrating both the wounded and the healing into one.

The journeyer is one who does not consciously slip into any one archetypal configuration, but who is fully present in the situation as it is. We do not deny either possibility but instead work with both to achieve the ultimate value, which is the presence of wholeness.

The Work

- *The victim, in your own words, is one who...*

- *What is a recent example of your playing victim in adult life?*

- *List your victim attitudes. Then rewrite these attitudes into affirmations to change them. What are the significant results?*

- *Describe your victim complex as best you can. Check it out with people who know you. Then picture and describe an image of greater wholeness for yourself.*

We do to ourselves what has been done to us.

38 God

Image: *The whirlwind hovers over a dry lake.*

'What is the religion of childhood?'

In childhood I had a relationship with God which lasted for years. God came in where my parents failed me. Where they were effective I did not need God.

From the earliest years until around age thirteen I had a bed wetting problem. I could not control my bladder when I fell asleep. Today this is one of the things which has made the night so powerful for me. In the night things happened, not of my own choosing. In the night I would be decisively defeated time after time. In the night it was only me against my unknown antagonist, God. And it was in the night that I learned to pray year after year for rescue by a new God, a God who never answered my prayers.

Almost every evening for three years I prayed to God not to wet the bed and almost every night I wet the bed. My parents hated it and tried and tried to figure out what to do. One vivid time I was put down for a nap at their friend's house and I wet right into the couch. I would wake up at boarding school, always too late, feeling the embarrassing clammy wetness. And I would stay awake for hours, rubbing dry sheet against wet, trying to get the sheet dry and the stains out so that no one would notice in the morning and I wouldn't be embarrassed once again.

There was no God in childhood for me. There was only a lonely, desperate boy's cry for help. Religion would have to be terribly real if this boy were later to accept it.

Many of us leave childhood either rejecting God as we reject the parents, or having been rejected by Him. We feel rejected by God because we were not saved from the worst of childhood, and in adult life we see more evil and destructiveness ahead. Many times when we seek religion and God we are looking for the healing relationship we feel we never got in childhood. We project the ideal parent onto our G-O-D image which becomes then the ideal parent in the sky. Religions themselves try to be the ideal family to their followers. Their leaders are idealised and have the role of giving and receiving love.

The first lesson of transforming childhood is to accept reality exactly as it is. To project parental longings onto a G-O-D image and onto a religious community and its leader is common and unwise. It takes us away from accepting life as it is and doing self-integration as our life task.

G-O-D may in fact exist as the prime mover of the universe and as a guiding force in our lives. But how will we ever find and relate to this Centrality if we are still in a state of projection onto a deity because we have not solved our childhood problems?

The Work

- *What is your earliest experience of God? Or what was your earliest or main spiritual experience in childhood? Write about it and its significance.*

- *How do you react to the above passage about this child's longing to be saved from wetting the bed? Why was he not saved?*

- *What is your present position regarding God and spiritual experience?*

- *What was your early childhood experience of your parents as God? Did they fail you or influence you in terms of your own spiritual experience? What is the child's general experience of God? Write a description of God from a child's point of view?*

- *If you pray, are these prayers of desperation or openness? Are you asking God to save you or meet your needs, as you would an ideal, all-powerful parent? Where did you get this parent–child concept of God? The only prayer is a prayer of openness, not demand. Practice this and see what happens.*

The presence of G-O-D is in the absence.

39 The Divine Child

Image: *The earth opens to reveal a new spring of water.*

'... the Great Gift, is the Divine Child ...'

And the angel of the Lord came upon them and said, 'Behold, this day is born to you a saviour who is Christ the Lord.' Within the Christian religion there are many beautiful Christmas hymns all focused on worshipping a Baby, a Divine Child.

What is this new birth, and why does it happen in the dead of winter? At the darkest time of the year many ancient religions celebrated the birth of a saviour, a divine child. It is also the time of miracles and light, as in the Jewish holiday of Hanukkah, the festival of lights.

Christmas as a cultural holiday has lasted centuries because it is based on a constellation of archetypes. Christmas comes around the time of the winter solstice, the darkest time of the year when the new light is born. A divine baby is an appropriate symbol for this event since it is the natural consequence of a union of opposites, the masculine and feminine. The holiday itself is an intersection of the archetypes of Death-Rebirth and the Journey, of cyclic time and historical, linear time.

The family archetype is especially prominent at this time with many people returning to their original families and stuffing themselves, trying to fill up again with parental sustenance to last a full year. Those not in a fulfilling relationship can become depressed. They may feel excluded from the family circle and the celebration of new life. If you cannot look forward to new life you are going to feel bad at a time when it is being most celebrated.

Your whole traumatic and needy childhood may emerge at Christmas and consequently you may feel depressed. Or you may feel like rushing around trying to preserve the family archetype by buying presents for everyone. Childhood was a needy time, a time in which you needed to be given to constantly. So in adult life each Winter Solstice millions of people go scurrying around trying to buy just the right present, attempting with gifts to fulfil needs never met in childhood. Watch your gift giving. How much of it is buying what you yourself want? You may have been taught to buy parental love by being good and now at Season's Greetings you again try to buy with gifts other people's love.

The only gift, the Great Gift, is the Divine Child, the possibility of new birth in the coming year, a birth which is at once unifying and personal to you and also new hope and growth for your culture and for the world.

The Christian Mandala

The Christian mandala occurs at the Winter Solstice, the darkest time of the year, the time of gestation and loss of light. A healing mandala is particularly needed at this time. Note that in our diagram we also include other primary religious symbols such as the snake of the Garden of Eden and Herod, the wicked king who tries to murder the Christ child. Traditional Christianity does not include Herod in the creche scene because it has a strong bias towards excluding rather than including evil as part of the total religious process. Since we are Jungian and use a wholeness perspective, we include the darkness very much present at the time of the birth of light.

The Work

- *What were your earliest winter celebrations like?*

- *What are your feelings and attitudes about giving gifts? What are you honestly doing? What would be a constructive inner attitude to follow in giving?*

- *How can you help the Divine Child be alive in you this year? This is meant as an archetype, not a religious figure. It does not have to be symbolised as it is in Christianity. If you paint the symbol, let it come naturally to you.*

- *What comes up for you in the Winter Solstice transition regarding the family archetype? How might you deal with these things? How has your family's celebration of the Winter Solstice influenced your life?*

Celebration is the heart's acceptance of healing and grace.

The Christian Mandala as represented in the Birth Story circa AD 300

40 A Six Year Old

Image: *A child looks out of the window.*

'... this my spirit you must keep.'

Who is this darling six year old who loves to play with me, ride piggy-back on my shoulders, and cries so easily if I am too rough with him? Such energy, such happiness, and such tears. My heart suffers with you when you fall off the slide and hurt yourself. You cannot control reality or your body, and painful things are happening to you. I cannot prevent some of these things.

You are a warm child, a bright child, full of the fun of life and always asking for things. Such energy keeps me moving and sometimes I cannot stand it anymore, and I have to say 'No' to you. You decide what you will and will not eat. I coax and command you but your will seems superior to my own. If I am to have my way, I will have to put out more energy than you and pay the consequences of your displeasure. You are not easy to defeat, even in your own interest, and I love you.

At night I put you to bed, tell you a story, sing you a song, and say with you a prayer I wrote.

> O God, as I go to sleep,
> this my spirit you must keep.
> Send a guardian angel from on high
> and give a dream as I lie.

I have modified the traditional image of childhood. I have made it not so dark for you and me. It no longer is, as in the traditional prayer, 'If I die before I wake, I pray the Lord my soul to take.' For you see, I want you to stay right here on earth. I do not want to lose you. You are my child. You are my hope. You are my inner delight and sadness, my creativity and vulnerability, my play and my spontaneity, my hope for the future and my lost past. I need you to be alive in me.

The Work

- *How do you respond to this description?*

- *Why not write a description of a six year old as it comes to you? You do not have to have an actual experience of a six year old. Think of yourself as a six year old, or just let your imagination take you where it will.*

- *What happened to you around age six? Perhaps there was some major transition or event? What was the essence, the 'life point' then?*

- *What is one way you sometimes act like a six year old now?*

- *Are you happy? Why? Why not? Are you defining happiness in terms of your childhood, or in terms of your more mature, adult years?*

We go to the child to find the adult.

41 Your Earliest Childhood Dream

Image: *A fire burns the landscape.*

'That earliest dream may be in a sense our destiny'

We remember from childhood what is of central importance to our personality. Within the psyche reside the patterns created in childhood. Let us then go to the dream, that reflection of the trembling myth in the inner world.

We went to our bed one night and had a great dream, a dream of major proportions which probably scared us awake. It was of such great intensity that we remember it still. This dream may have repeated itself in one form or another throughout our childhood. Perhaps its symbols and themes still come into our dreams in adult life.

What is possible is that the remembered dream from childhood is one which reflects our personal myth, a basic pattern which we have been living out all our lives. Was it that tiger trying to get into the room with two doors? We would go to one door and hold it closed, and the tiger would go to the other door and try to enter to devour us. In adult life such a dream would reflect a constant fear of invasion, and insufficient ability to cope with life's stresses. To find healing the dreamer can re-enter the dream as an adult and help that little child deal with the tiger. What are the alternatives? Leave the situation and try to find a room with only one door? Go out of the room, and face the tiger and see what it wants? Let the tiger in and make friends with it, and use its power for new life? Let the tiger in and let oneself be devoured in the dream state and see what happens next?

First we look at the basic pattern reflected in the dream. In this example life is seen as scary and dangerous, and the dreamer's reaction to this fear is to engage in defensive action rather than change a fundamental attitude that powerful things will destroy you. Then we must reflect on how the dream has been lived out in one's outer life. With the person who dreamed of the tiger her anger and relations with men were often overpowering for her.

By working with the dream, we can change defeating patterns and attitudes to more effective and healing ones. That earliest dream may

The Nightmare

be in a sense our destiny, our problem to solve before we can be free to fulfil ourselves in adult life.

Every life situation is in fact a double bind situation. Any energy can go either way in life and often choices make all the difference. As in the dream, you may not be able to keep the tiger out, but you can sometimes choose by which door he or she is to enter. And you can even choose the door by which you will exit when things become impossible.

The Work

- *Write up your earliest childhood dream, first the basics you remember and then an elaboration or fuller imaginative description of it.*

- *What does your childhood dream say about yourself as a child? What is the pattern there? Is it resolved, brought to completion, or is resolution still needed? How has the pattern in the dream been acted out throughout your life?*

- *Do a dream re-entry with your eyes closed. See the dream again and experience it, but this time bring in the 'adult you' and help the 'child you' so that new feelings and imagery appear in order to bring completion. If this is hard or fearful for you, ask someone skilled to guide you through the dream. Or rewrite the dream, bringing it to resolution. What is significant about the resolution which comes? Elaborate, then write down some commitments for change in your life based on changes in the dream.*

We are the dream dreaming us.

42 Death in the Family

Image: *A gate blowing in the wind.*

'If you can face death you can face life.'

Death ... Death in the family. It may have been only a little one, or it may have been very close to you. Your father or your mother, your brother or your sister. Possibly a grandparent or some other relative. Perhaps you did not know death directly this early in childhood. Yet somehow death entered your consciousness and provoked in you the ultimate questions.

Do all things die? Is so-and-so gone forever? Where do things go when they put them in the ground?

Possibly these questions came to you more from the little things. The dead beetle in the back garden. Your pet dog that died a natural death, or was run over by a car. This recognition of absence, of mortality, is one of the births for the ego. The slim small ego of the child recognises that some day it will be no more. There is at this age a certain clarity about one's place in the universe which often becomes muddled in the adult years with neurosis, egocentrism, identification with the world, and scientific and religious doctrines about reality.

At what age did this question of death hit you and how did you survive it? Are you still afraid of death? Re-entering your childhood experience of death, like you would re-enter a dream, can help you come to terms with death. In death there may be new life, but there is no return to the old.

In childhood death seems far away, almost absent. Therefore many of us remain identified with being a child. We don't want the years to creep up on us, chopping away at our substance, and finally taking us in the end. But perhaps we are not ready to die because we have not yet lived. We grew up too soon, and now as adults we pursue the lost childhood, hoping to avoid death until our childhood has found us.

Some of us were taught by adults to avoid death. There was a death in the family and someone in authority decided that the little children should not be there at the funeral service. Nobody talked to us, people hid things from our ears.

Death for most adults is not the mystery it is for the natural child. If you can face death you can face life. For in each moment resides the choice to live or die. How we choose in the little things makes all the difference. In order to live we must die. We must sacrifice the old values, the worn-out ways of doing things, in order to practise a new potential. Life is the goal of life and dying the process. Why not become that child again who wakes to each new day having to let go of the old?

The Work

- *Describe your early fundamental experience of death. Even if it was of someone very close to you, tell yourself about it once again, and in a way that sees death as natural and necessary to life. Not death, the great deprivation, but death, the teacher of my destiny. What has this childhood death experience to teach me?*

- *What is your present view of death? In what ways might it be influenced by early childhood experience?*

- *What, if any, connections between God and death did you make in childhood?*

- *We do not fear death if we have found life. Write your response to this statement. Write with flowing and feeling!*

Death gives life to life as life gives life to death.

43 The Soul

Image: *Into the pool a stone drops.*

'Does individuality survive death?'

Far away, even millions of light years away, abide the endless configurations of souls, the essences of those who have come and gone. Or do they still reside surrounding us, layer upon concentric layer, as near infinite sparks of being which once were in the flesh?

Does individuality survive death? We may not know how to respond to that question. And yet throughout our lives many of us know transcendence. We experience mysterious and strange things, things far greater than ourselves. In this sense the child knows more than the adult. For the child is soul, that essence which has not yet been fully accepted and merged into concrete life.

The soul is the spark of the eternal, the relation between a person and the Source. The Source transcends life yet gives life meaning. The soul is that which transcends death, yet, unless we have worked to have our souls transcend life, the spark will be pitiful indeed.

There is no bank in heaven. You spend now and learn what you are doing. You can develop an enduring perspective outside yourself. The soul is what detaches us from life.

Return to childhood. Return to childhood now, the first phase of experiencing soul. Perhaps you knew it all before you arrived. Your soul, your unique essence, may or may not have wanted to be born in the flesh.

Suddenly you found yourself alive and in a body. And you spent many years thus limited and excited by life. And still you had those transcendent experiences, those chorales of eternity, of deep knowing, that you would struggle a life-time to put into action. You would elude your soul but it would not elude you.

Somehow you could not be completely who the others thought you were. You had experiences, you knew that there was more to life than 'they' seemed to be conveying to you. You were a stranger in their midst and they were trying to reach out for you, to make you one of them.

The soul knows no boundaries. Prepare! Let go, let go a long way. When the birth is all over you will have begun.

The Work

- *Are you one of those who eagerly embraced coming into a body and being born? Are you one who loves life and wants to be here? Or do you feel yourself to be one of the reluctant ones who came to planet earth but never quite fit in? Does the world seem limiting? Do you long for much more than what seems to have fallen to your lot? Did you want entry into your body or do you feel it more as a forced choice upon you? What do you suppose explains your reluctance? How are you dealing with it now? What progress have you made in making your compromise with reality?*

- *What are you doing now at a daily level to develop your soul, the eternal and essential part of yourself? What sacrifices are perhaps necessary to free your soul from too much worldly life? Do you feel there is a World Soul, a powerful entity which wants your soul to bond with it?*

In the silences we are most real.

44 The Collective

Image: *The king sits on his old throne.*

'The collective is all those rules, values and attitudes by which the group lives.'

When I wake up in the morning, whose person am I? I was born into this world and immediately it laid its claim on me. The world wanted me for its own, and all too often I acquiesced. What was I to do? I had my needs and the world would meet my needs if I conformed to its expectations. For security I often gave up my individual self. For security I paid a price of conforming to the image of what a nice baby was to them.

I acted like them, so they thought I was one of them, and then met my needs. What was I to do? I was only a baby who had to have help to grow up in this world. Fairly soon I began to see the world as they did, to do the things they thought important.

I had lost almost all sense of myself when they failed to meet my needs. The suffering they caused me made me realise that I was still an individual after all. I could not totally merge with the state, the religion, the group, the family. I was one individual in the world. I would have to figure out how to meet more of my own needs and try to understand this collective of which I was a part.

The collective is all those rules, values and attitudes by which the group lives. It is also the view of reality held by a culture and its people. On the inner plane, the collective is the attitudes and values within us from parents and society, as well as the archetype of the group.

To rebel against the collective may be a necessary stage, but one nevertheless that is still very much tied to the collective, if only in reaction to it.

Rebellion creates the edge, the new emphasis in society for tomorrow. One generation rebels against the former by living out in a new way the shadow of the previous generation. We go from long hair to short hair, from looseness of attitude to highly structured attitudes, and so on. Each shadow lives itself out and creates a new shadow for the next generation to rebel against. This helps progress if it does not become an endless swinging back and forth.

To become an individual we must disidentify from either merger or rebellion against the collective. We make peace with the collective, making conscious its values and world view, and working within it to achieve our own productivity and wholeness. Rebellion does not create a new identity, it creates an individual at war with the world an him or herself. The true individual is formed out of a unity of all the parts within and without.

In the same way, we must neither stay identified with inner dynamics nor flee from them by focusing strictly on the outer world. To individuate, we work to integrate both inner and outer.

At some point, because we are not identified with it, we emerge from the group a leader. People see in us a special quality. We have free energy for living at the edge of new possibilities.

We can be sacrificed by the collective or become the focus for its deepest aspirations and next development.

The Work

- *What figure in history represents most for you what individuality is? What qualities especially appeal to you? How might these also be in you?*

- *What has been your history in relating to the collective? Merger? Rebellion? Other? What is your present relation to your own inner collective, your unconscious? In what ways are you willing to be an individual in this life?*

What we leave unconscious rules us.

45 Processing the Void

Image: *The snail has burst its shell.*

'Meet terror and die to a defended life.'

Maybe you have not experienced it but in childhood there can come to certain children an experience which feels like the loss of reality.

Perhaps you wake up from a nap but find that you cannot move your body. Or in the night you experience indescribable terror. The walls move ... the floor gives way ... the ceiling is falling in on you. What started as a dream breaks through in waking life also.

Beyond our known limits of reality stands the void. All our activities and immersion in the everyday world keep back the utter darkness. When the known images of who we are, of who we identify as ourselves, dissolve then we experience the swirling void of lostness. We literally do not know who we are or on what firm ground we can stand.

As children we resist the void. We try to flee from it to our mother's arms. Soft warm flesh is human. We hide from the void in our fantasies of hero and heroine. We do little rituals to keep back the face of the deep.

As adults our worlds may fall apart from time to time, and again we experience the void. But this time we can, if we know how, process the void by plunging into it.

Flight from the void into the known will not help us with our ultimate fears. Facing the nothingness behind the surface of concrete and emotional reality will give us the solidity to take on almost anything in life. And why not? What we most fear will happen anyway. Each of us, through the great gateway of death, will enter the forever point. Better to face the empty darkness while still alive, the more to savour the fullness of life. Facing the darkness is an ultimate task for one who would master fate.

Return to childhood then. It never ends happily, contrary to all the folk tales that children must hear in order to sleep at night. Return to childhood. The healing process demands that you become utterly defenceless, no longer fighting adversity. And you can do it within a nest of healing, someone's loving but firm arms, the therapist's commitment, the spiritual teacher's challenge and acceptance. Then you can make transition to new life.

Too many adults look strong for their age while underneath, hidden in a bag of sorrow, screams the inner child.

Let go and suffer, and live, and heal, facing the void, the absolute terror which makes us feel so insignificant and small. Face it now with tears and affirmations. There cannot be any more terror until you have met the terror there is. Meet terror and die to a defended life. Meet terror and purge yourself of fear. When the shattering is done and the void passes, new life will have begun, a flowering seed present in the soil of the earth, the emotion of caring, the reality of knowing you have made it through this time.

The Work

- *What was your most terrifying experience of utter nothingness in childhood? Describe in detail so that your pattern for dealing with darkness can become clear.*

- *What today is your experience of ultimate darkness? How does it relate to your childhood experience?*

- *Re-experience, if you can, a childhood experience of the void, but this time bring the adult you into the situation to help your inner child feel secure in dealing with the experience. Do not save the child. Support it in confronting the void.*

- *Re-experience your most recent experience of the void, one in which you were not in control and felt no known boundaries or resources at your disposal. This time do not resist the experience in any way, but go through it to strengthen your ego. Make sure you have competent support available in case you get overwhelmed.*

- *Do a meditation on the void, contemplate it and see what moves in you. In contemplating the void, experience any fears which come up. Behind all your relative fears is probably one great fear. Experience this directly and go through it. What is it like? What becomes resolved?*

- *Paint the void in an imaginative way.*

We most fear that which has not yet become known.

46 Peers

Image: *Five apples and a pear have fallen from the same tree.*

'I had to fit in, for I felt my life depended on it.'

My example is unusual but vivid. Strange as it may seem, at home I was not allowed to play with other children my age in those earliest years of my childhood. Then at age six I was sent away to boarding school, never to return home again, except for short yearly vacations. There I had to fit in, for I felt my life depended on it. There was always the group bully, like the little Italian kid I feared and appeased. There were also those who liked me and with whom I could form friendships. In those early years I was never the leader when we played games of war or hide and seek. I did not feel liked enough to be a leader, but I made an excellent assistant to the leader. I would run errands fast, and make good suggestions for strategy.

Things changed when I was sent to military school at age twelve. There leadership was only partly based on outgoing friendliness. The military had hundreds of obvious standards to be measured by. I made good grades, trained well at military drill and worked hard. I received promotions, class presidencies, and respect in certain quarters. I also made enemies, all those who were my competitors for the rewards. I learned to fear how the group mood could change and pounce on each one of us in turn.

The times when I was alone, or with only one other friend I could trust, were the best times, the most secure. The outer collective seemed too powerful and fickle to trust. In my late teens and twenties I became a rebel and feared the collective even more. My peers were both hell and heaven on earth. We both hated each other and soothed each other's wounds. We had fun, we played, and dreamed of a world we would someday control.

My heart goes out to my brothers and sisters everywhere. We are on a rocky boat together. We must cooperate with the collective. Our peers are a part of us. United we can change the world.

The Work

- *You are in the early ages of childhood, say the period of six,*

112

seven and eight years old. You already have an idea of what the parents and society want. But you are spending most of your time doing your own thing with little people your own age. What is it they want? What are the power dynamics within the group? What are their values? How have you suffered by not knowing how to fit into your group? Yes, you will go to parents and teachers for help, but they cannot be there to guard you all the time. You must seek allies within your own society. You are the next generation. Write about this experience as it happened to you.

- *What kind of persona, or outer image of who you are, did you construct to get along with your peers? How did this change over the years?*

- *These days, what is your relation to a group? Your fears? How do you cope with groups? Why do you need groups?*

- *How do you get along with people of either sex of your own age? What does this tend to say about yourself?*

No boat is safe on a tumultuous sea.

47 The Road Not Taken

Image: *Travellers resting at a wayside inn.*

'In life, there are always at least two roads we travel.'

T.S. Eliot gives a wonderful metaphor in a poem. He describes a magical garden somewhere which we can visit, where resides all the choices and paths contemplated but not taken. What then do we do with the unlived life? What would I be like today if only childhood had been different?

Return to childhood? What unlived life is still back there waiting to be born? If only my mother had not died or disappeared when I was six or my father had not left when I was eight? Or if only I had a sister or a brother, or not had a sister or brother? What is your magical childhood like?

In life, there are always at least two roads we travel. The outer one of actual accomplishment in physical reality, and the imaginary-archetypal one of inner reality. If we were condemned to live life only in the outer, where would we be? Most of us deny that the inner world is as real as the outer, and so we neglect it, not realising that often experiences of archetypal reality have as much or more meaning as those which occur in the outer.

Scratch an adult and you get a child, a human being who is living out a magical kingdom of 'what should have been' while dealing on the outside with the affairs of the world. Let us acknowledge the inner kingdom of fantasy for what it is and then let it go. Our goal, our health, is to live in the 'here and now', not in a 'reality' we would have liked. Yet take the magic, and fantasy, and honour it in thought and feeling by doing inner work around it which might actually lead to outer expression. You cannot live your childhood again, but can redeem the past by acting differently in the present.

The Work

- *What are some of the roads not taken for you? Explore and describe.*

- *Ideally, how would you have liked those early years to have been? Describe in detail and let your feelings come up.*

114

• *Explore and even write down your current fantasies. How might they be replicating childhood fantasies? What unlived life resides in those fantasies? What is the essence, the necessity, which you need to express more in present life? Look to your fantasies to signal needed life expression.*

• *See to what extent your present fantasising is keeping you from being fully in the moment in present life. How can you enliven your present life with the energy behind your fantasies?*

• *How free are you from identification with outer reality? What percent of your day do you spend on inner matters? What changes are needed to strike a balance?*

• *Paint a picture, or a symbolic map, of childhood as you would have liked it to have been.*

The life we live redeems the unlived life.

48 The Secret Sin

Image: *A bear stalks the outer meadow.*

'True confession brings resolution, not absolution.'

Each of us is hiding something from the world. Is it time to reveal that secret now? Is there anything about yourself which you have told no one in your life? Is it actually so terrible that it cannot be revealed?

Let us begin with the secret life of the child. There were so many prohibitions that we just had to break a few of them. Or were we one of those who never let ourselves get out of hand, even in little things, for fear we would be caught?

The secret of keeping a secret is that secrets preserve a certain image. If what I have done is unacceptable to others, it is likely to be unacceptable to myself. I confess my sins to accept them myself. True confession brings resolution, not absolution. We remain responsible to ourselves for what we have done. It does not go away into the chalice of forgiveness. It becomes more a part of ourselves. The great secret is the shadow, the seamy part of our personalities which gets acted out against our better judgement.

At military school when I was thirteen, I inadvertently stole something. Through my years of boarding school, I had maintained a rigid system of honesty, so afraid was I of being caught and severely punished. I must have reasoned that since I was regularly punished with other boys for acts I did not commit, I was even worse off if I did commit any.

It was at the end of the school year and we went through the rooms of those boys who did go home for the summer, to see if there was anything of value that they had voluntarily left behind. One room was a treasure trove and I found an object I especially liked and took it, only the owner came back the next day to claim his belongings and caused an extraordinary fuss. I never did return what I had taken, and I thus became for this one time a thief in childhood. My shadow had received an acknowledgement and I felt as guilty as possible.

The more identified we are with our personas, the bright image of ourselves, the more compulsive becomes that which we reject about ourselves. To confess and mean it is to accept the shadow, not to give it away. Where will the shadow go if we do not take it in?

We have to hide sins for fear of the collective. If we were found out it would not go well with us. Yet we must create our sins to disidentify from the collective. What others consider sin may be what we need for integration.

And in adult years what would we like to keep hidden? The story of the shadow and its intrigues continues. What is one person's value is another person's sin. Elusive as the secret is, we must find it and reveal it to ourselves. Sometimes this means revealing it to others as well.

From the point of view of individuation, we are not so much interested in the acts of sin as we are in what lies behind them. What need, what archetype, is so coursing through our soul that it must seek expression in what is forbidden?

The Work

- *List your darkest secrets from childhood, even the ones which you have told no one. What archetypal and personal energy might be behind them?*

- *If you do not seem to have much in the way of childhood sins, then list some close encounters where you wish that you had gone against the collective's values.*

- *List acts which make you doubt yourself or feel bad. In what ways do you feel the need to act against your own values or those of the collective?*

- *Is any sin unredeemable? What is redemption psychologically and spiritually?*

To sin is to honour life with our imperfection!

The Secret

49 Money

Image: *The sapphire in the light of the moon has brought the night closer.*

'Money is a fiction. We are the reality.'

The things of the world may rot and break apart but money remains forever. Money has no ties. It stays with an owner only so long as it is possessed. The owner dies and the money lives on. Money has no charity nor any principles. It does both harm and good. It resists nothing, not even itself. Men will die for it while it remains alive. We possess money and are possessed by it. Money seeks its own. It lies in vaults and secret places. It works not except for itself. It's uses are many yet it has no use of its own. It can claim nothing, neither a place to lie down or a house to live in, yet without money there are few who can shelter themselves.

Money does not love, yet many have sold and bought love with money. Where money is lacking there also is love lacking. Love survives on money but money hardly survives on love.

Money is not honest. It does not respond and reward us if we are good. Money does not give us a good time if we have lots of it, nor does it create happiness.

Money does not make us sick or deprive us. It is not what makes life hard for us. Money does not prepare us for death or give us the right friends. It is not the value for which life has been created.

Money does not complain or sulk when we get angry. Nor does it heal us when we are sick.

Money is power without choice, and what we choose to do with money reflects the values by which we live.

The key to prosperity is doing what is necessary to conserve our resources for both the up and the down times. For there will surely be dry periods as well as the full in this existence. Another key is to keep a positive attitude towards developing the potential that is actually there in life. The third principle is to find and do what is in tune with our true nature and the world around us. Money is the fiction. We are the reality.

119

The Work

- *What were your earliest experiences of money? What attitudes were created for you by these experiences?*

- *What were each of your parent's attitudes towards money? How have these attitudes been acted out by you in your own life? What psychological and spiritual dynamics and principles might have been behind these parental attitudes?*

- *What of the above statements in the text did you respond to? What were your inner voices saying to you as you read the passage?*

- *Read the passage to a friend, or even a parent, and get their reaction. Use it as a basis for discussion and consciousness raising.*

- *What is the chief point, as you understand it, of our approach to money in this lesson?*

- *What is the most creative and dynamic position you can take personally towards money in your life? What will you do to manifest this position?*

Money measures our perception of reality.

50 Dependency

Image: *The umbilical cord is wrapped around the baby's neck.*

'Dependency is the shadow side of seeking fulfilment.'

We all know the scourge of dependency in adult life. We depend on someone and then they fail us. We feel betrayed and hurt and may even vow not to depend on anyone ever again. Should there even be dependency in adult life? Or is this another one of those left-over issues from childhood?

Real dependency is necessary. There are times when I might as an adult need to seek financial or medical help. There are also times when I might need to seek therapeutic help.

Feigned dependency has some hidden motive. I am dependent when I expect you to do something for me. I am dependent when I am unable to do something for myself. I am dependent when I believe you will meet a need of mine because you said you would. I am dependent when I want you to contribute in some way to my welfare. I am dependent when I expect things for which I have not worked.

On the other hand, do I let go of my control whenever I seek help? Do I let myself be nurtured and supported? Some of us feel no one can do the job as well as we can. So we do not ask others to do anything for us because they might not meet our standards. This attitude can create its own form of dependency since we deny to ourselves the help that is naturally there from others and the universe. We over-depend on ourselves.

In neurotic dependency we manipulate or demand that our needs be met by others. The worst dependency is that of identification with the victim archetype. This is the hardest to self-cure because victim types believe that their wounds are greater than their ability to cure them. They manipulate others to see themselves as victims needing help. The piece missing in this puzzle is back in childhood. The child was in fact helpless and had to play helpless to get at least some of its needs met.

It would have been better for me and for everyone else who has had to deal with me, if more of my needs had been met. But they were not met and that is reality. No one has to meet my needs in this life.

121

People are concerned with their own needs. We meet our needs ourselves by tapping into healing places through our own choices and consciousness.

The dependency problem in adulthood is apparent when we hang around other people still demanding like a child to have our needs met. If this is an abundant universe, then go out and fulfil yourself. When you have a need only someone else can meet, present your need as a gift to them so that they will themselves be meeting a need of their own. And pay back your debts by learning to give to yourself what others first had to give to you.

Do not depend on others. Do not depend on yourself alone. In place of dependency put mutual creation. Your parents never met your needs fully, did they? And you survived. What was the secret?

The Work

- *List some areas in your present life in which you feel compulsively dependent on someone or on a particular situation. What is your earliest recollection of being thus dependent? What shifts can you make?*

- *List some ways you feel too independent in adult life, in the sense that you will not let anyone help you or partake with you in the activity? What insecurity or attitudes might be behind this?*

We are dependable when we are not dependent.

51 My Favourite Teacher

Image: *The wren brings worms to its nestlings.*

'Without this one, this significant other, what would I be today?'

An old but vivid memory is taking me back many years. Miss Day was a communist, or so my parents told me years later. This meant that although it was all right to be a communist during the Second World War, she was later fired from her job as third-grade teacher of my boarding school.

The school was such a cold place to live, mainly because no one cared about me. I was just one of hundreds of children. Although they may have cared about all of us together, they could not take a warm interest in each one of us. But Miss Day cared for me. I felt that from the first. After the horrors of the night and dormitory life I would go off to school and there find acceptance.

Miss Day appears to me now as a bright sun, a warm sun on a cloudy planet. Learning is always a challenge for me, and she must have offered me warmth and acceptance for the mistakes I made, as well as praise for my accomplishments.

The significance for me is that somewhere in the crowd of all those people who were entrusted with my growth and upbringing, one cared for me as a person. Without this one, this significant other, what would I be today? I could not have her as my mother, but her genuineness as a person gave me hope in enduring those dark years of childhood until I could be an adult myself.

The message I got from Miss Day is that there were warm people in the world capable of love, and that if I would make it through childhood, I would find them when I had the power to guide my own life.

And find them I did. Abundantly!

The Work

- *What feelings and memories have come up for you now regarding a significant person early in your life? What is their meaning, their healing?*

- *Who was your favourite teacher in childhood, and why? Describe.*

- *What aspects of the parental archetypes might your favourite teachers have filled out for you?*

- *What did the terrible teachers contribute to your life?*

- *Which is easier for you, to learn from books or to have someone else convey the information personally to you? What basis in your own childhood experience might your predisposition have come from?*

What we need to learn in life will be taught to us one way or another.

52 School

Image: *A red and white ball tossed high in the air.*

'What we most learned, or did not learn, in school is how to learn.'

What feelings does the word 'school' bring up for you? I feel 'school' as an anxious challenge, a situation in which constant demands are put on me to control my behaviour and learn, learn, learn.

What we most learned, or did not learn, in school is how to learn. What are my attitudes in adult life towards taking in new things? What image do I have of myself as a competent learner? This is determined for better and for worse by my early study experiences.

One incident comes to mind which has coloured my whole life. I was having difficulty learning how to spell. I would be sent out of class with two girls to learn the assignment for the day. I didn't like girls at that age, and I learned to hate spelling. Getting a word wrong was considered the end of the world for me, a lack of perfection. It meant being laughed at and made to feel inferior, getting singled out in the group, being made to do extra work until I got the words right. My anxiety was always at a high level. I was in no way relaxed, and this made memorising difficult.

Today, as an adult I do not spell well. But I have a love of words, and I am much more accepting of my own imperfection. I can laugh when someone points out a spelling error on my part. I have still created something real, even if it is misspelled.

And I do work to improve my spelling, trying to figure out why a word is spelled one way and not another. It is not the word I misspell, but the real anxiety about life which gets expressed, so I deal with that. It has become almost fun to redeem my childhood a little more with each new word I spell with confidence and not anxiety.

The key experience in adult life which comes directly from our early study is The Test, and the great anxiety this seems to produce in most of us. Typically we wake with a dream of not being prepared for an examination, or on stage and we have forgotten our lines. This reflects an archetypal situation in which we are challenged by a life opportunity or situation and dissolve in fear because we feel we lack the necessary information and resources to meet the challenge effectively. In school we studied for the exam, but not enough, and we almost failed. Daily in this life we are under challenge to meet the next crisis or opportunity and to deal with it successfully. Until we learn how to meet challenge we will miss out on many of the most important things of life. The lesson from school is not the lesson. It is life. To be successful you must overcome your anxiety in any situation and use the resources available to bring resolution. Do not hesitate for long or life will pass you by. Better to fail than not to participate at all. But to succeed has the sweetest joy. If you did not get this in school, learn it now by studying the art of effectiveness.

To be effective we must open ourselves to a situation just as it is. Accept the situation, see its difficulties and opportunities, then choose that which has the greatest potential for resolution and new life. Do not hesitate. Make the decisive choices. Sacrifice all which stands in the way of the new choice, deal with the outcomes, and never look back.

The Work

- *What are the major issues, attitudes, and self-images you picked up from school?*

- *Take one area or issue from your school experience and write about it. Describe your experience and the images, feelings, and attitudes it created in you. What, if any, have been the transformations in adult life?*

- *How would you describe your present learning pattern? Is it effective? Has it been cleansed of negative conditioning left over from childhood? What needs further work?*

Living to learn must be balanced by learning to live.

53 The Great Betrayal!

Image: *The well is full of water but the pump is broken.*

'Innocence is the prerogative of the child and the danger of
the adult.'

Somewhere in the passages of time we were defeated, even
devastated. We were betrayed. Our faith in another person or in the
world was destroyed, and thank God it was! Reality is a good cure for
prolonged innocence. Innocence is the prerogative of the child and the
danger of the adult.

'But you said you would.'

'It's not fair.'

'I trusted you!'

'I assumed you were going to do it.'

'People should be nice to each other.'

'Nobody lets me down and gets away with it.'

Have you ever said any of these statements? Do you still say some
of them, or other statements like them?

Everyone has felt more or less betrayed in childhood. Yet there can
be no betrayal unless there is innocence. 'Yes, they hurt me and it
wasn't fair' you say. Of course it wasn't fair. And whoever said the
world was fair? Your parents? You? God? Where did you ever get the
idea that this was a just world with principles of right and wrong
which people followed?

As a child you expected the world to be fair and just. You felt
betrayed when you experienced unfairness, and wanted things to be
different. The point is that these things were not different even
though you didn't deserve them.

You had a very hard time accepting that you were the recipient of
injustice and imperfection, and your young inner child has probably
not got over it yet.

Perhaps you were fair and could be trusted. But be honest, if you
were being the most good, weren't you manipulating your situation a

little by being well thought of so as to avoid the heat of deprivation which might come your way?

Perhaps even today you believe in such things as trust and commitment. You keep all your commitments even though others don't always keep theirs. You can be trusted. If you say you will do something, you will, won't you? And basically you are fair? You wouldn't dream of meeting your own ends first. Of course not? Then why does it make you angry when someone else does not come through and fails you? Is there some hidden obligation that if you are good to others, others should be good to you?

In adult years we may still expect people to meet our needs and communicate with us in just and honourable ways. Perhaps they will. Accept them if they do, but expect nothing. Deal with life, don't moralise. If others consciously or unconsciously go against your needs and values, deal with this by becoming a little wiser and more worldly in the uses of power.

For trust, substitute consciousness. A person may come through or not come through with what you consider the right behaviour. Are you going to sit around lamenting your fate, or get on with the living of life?

Perhaps the greatest inhibitor to a fully vital and adult life is the betrayal that one felt in childhood and the defensive personality which was built up around this event.

Find healing in accepting that adversity is a part of being alive in this reality. We need adversity to cure us of innocence. Accept betrayal, not with unrelated forgiveness, but with an increased reality function, so that you may become truly effective in life.

There is nothing to forgive. Reality does not admit of false judgements of right and wrong. The people we at first thought good all had their shadows. You do not forgive someone or something. What happens, happens. It is done. Learn from it. That is your redemption. You learn that all people, including yourself, have shadows. You stay aware of everyone's potential for destructiveness. You accept the shadow and move on.

The Work

- *What reactions are you experiencing by reading the above passage? Try to get at them and express them. What attitudes have been challenged?*

- *What is your position on trust? How has trust actually worked in your life? How has it been effective? How has it not been effective?*

- *What was the great betrayal for you in childhood? Try to feel it by holding the images surrounding the betrayal in your meditative state until the feelings come out. Then accept those feelings. What attitudes were being shattered at the time? What was the teaching behind the event?*

- *What defences towards the possibility of new betrayal did you build up in childhood which might still be in effect today?*

- *There are many adults who complain that someone has betrayed them, and that it is the other person's fault that they feel badly. No one fails anyone else. We fail only ourselves. Please write about this. Perhaps there is someone still out there in your world towards whom you have anger for not being the way you wanted them to be. Try to accept them into your meditation and see-feel them both as your betrayer and your saviour. Yes, saviour. The goal as an adult is to take full responsibility for accepting the imperfections which come your way. If you can begin to do this you will be on your way towards accepting your own imperfections.*

The only betrayal is the loss of consciousness in the face of reality.

54 The Anima

The image: *The bald priestess has laid her shorn hair at the foot of the altar.*

'She breaks all bonds and establishes new ones.'

The anima is the wild feminine energy inside every man which humbles him when he becomes too rational and too identified with his own masculine nature. She is wildly exciting, full of nuance. She is juice and mystery, acted out in fantasy, in nature, on many a couch and in many a story or poem. She breaks all bonds and establishes new ones.

The man's anima is sometimes at war with the woman's own feminine nature. For if the woman is always embodying the man's anima for him, she will be neglecting the expression of her own feminine which is sometimes different from the man's projected feminine. A man may project his feminine as a nurturing mother energy onto a woman who finds painting the most natural expression of her own feminine. If she is only concerned with embodying the man's feminine by cooking and caring for him, she will not be expressing *her* true feminine.

Anima projection may happen in a father-daughter relationship as well. The young woman is the young wife-woman resurrected for the father-man. Death will be approaching with the years and new young life is seen as the symbol of eternity. The father or step-father feels drawn to the young daughter. She symbolises and acts out his feelings for him. She may manipulate him through feeling to get some of her needs met. If the projection becomes too powerful at puberty, her father, or even her brother, will turn on her. She is a woman, a sexual being they must reject for fear of incest. She who has been happy embodying the feminine then withdraws, perplexed that such beauty she has been given has produced lust and raw anger. Anima fixation is not a happy sight.

When is the man's anima much younger than he is? If a man is attracted to younger women, if the beautiful women of his dreams are younger than he is, then his masculine conscious side is older than his feeling and feminine side. Since he has devoted so much more of his life to developing his masculine side, he has neglected his feminine, leaving it underdeveloped and immature.

130

For a man the way to the feminine is not by keeping the anima projected onto certain women, but to take back the projections and develop the feeling-relational function. We integrate by turning the energy of projections into functions. This way we develop a new side of ourselves symbolised by the projection. A man who tends to project mother onto women can nurture himself, cook for himself at least once in a while, take care of his own body instead of always needing a woman's caress to make him feel good.

On the other hand, a *woman* can learn not to identify totally with the anima, yet not reject it. The woman who is uncomfortable with her own feminine will not be comfortable receiving the man's anima projection. She will be out of touch with this powerful aspect of relatedness between the sexes. The sexes project energies onto each other, and this needs to be honoured and handled with care while at the same time helping the projections to be integrated.

When women feel mistreated by men they may use the power generated by the anima projection against the man to gain control over him. I will never forget seeing a beautiful friend of mine walking quickly into a coffee house with an ardent male trailing six steps behind her.

Eros is for relatedness, not power. The attractions of the sexes can be used to build beautiful and growing companionships, or they can be used in a power game of both trying to control the other. If in childhood you had to manipulate the natural projections which were aroused then the chances are you will be doing the same thing in your adult relationships. Break the chain. Integrate. Choose to be with someone who not only loves you but who integrates much of what love can mean.

Let both sexes be guardians of the feminine.

The Work

- *As a woman, what was your childhood pattern in embodying the man's anima, first with the father, or brother, and then later with boys?*

- *As a woman, what of your feminine have you developed for yourself that is not connected with attracting the man's anima?*

- *For the man, write a history of your anima. List the woman you loved. Remember them all. What were the qualities you were projecting onto these women? What realisations do you come to now?*

131

- *For the man, what of your anima projection are you now beginning to integrate and express as your own feminine side?*

- *For the man, did anyone in childhood accuse you of being homosexual or effeminate? What was behind it?*

- *For the man or woman, what were your experiences, fantasies, and attitudes about homosexuality in terms of the feminine or masculine?*

- *Make a plan and a commitment for dealing with the anima!*

Integrating love's potential creates the ability to love.

55 Sibling Rivalry

Image: *The chicks cry in the nest.*

'The losers in the power game need to learn that they too can succed, can have fulfilment more than denial.'

Once when I was working with a woman in her mid thirties, I had the image of attacking her breasts. I thought, why not? Why not act on it? She was aware of insecurity problems dating back to childhood. We were doing process training and in process training anything goes. I suddenly started poking at her breasts. She defended herself, of course, with a mixture of rage and tears. She also got the immediate insight of her brother doing that to her for years as they were growing up. So there it was, her early trauma in playing the power game. It was sexual and yet it was more basic than sexual. For sexuality, or either sex, can and must be a vulnerable experience.

This woman needed to get her fighting spirit up, she needed to go from an insecure defensive posture to one of true assertiveness. She could still be sexual and let go to vulnerability and love energy, but only because now she knew how to defend herself successfully. She need never feel as insecure again. She no longer needed to be the victim, and she had found the uses of her own effectiveness.

There is little protection against ones brothers and sisters or other children of a similar age. Generally speaking, we attack that which makes us feel insecure. The victims know what it is like for someone to dominate them in order to feel safe. The only way to have power is to take it. No one in this life gives their power away. *You must be willing to win in order not to lose.* Not everything in this life works by co-operation and good will. We must each fight for our space and be tested and proved worthy of the power we demand. Fulfilment is the fundamental need.

Take your stand and make your actions conscious. Study the manipulations of others and refuse to play their games. Go after what you need to fulfil yourself, you will be a better person for it, and for others who relate to you, but do not manipulate others. Power is effectiveness so, test all your ideals and attitudes. Effectiveness is the true test of reality. Until the woman relaxed her body and her mind under the attack on her breasts, and focused her spirit and physical energy for a shove and a strong voice that said, *Stop!* she would never find her right place in the structures of life.

The Work

- *What was the most evocative aspect for you about the above material? What issues did it bring up for you?*

- *Note the ability to act on intuition I used to help cause a breakthrough. We often know that something important is present in a situation, but until we are willing to act on our intuitions we will not be effective at the breakthrough level in life. What attitudes are needed for you to operate from a healing intuition?*

- *Make a drawing or diagram of the power relations in your childhood. What power did you have? How did you win it? How was some of your natural power taken from you? This is important in order to participate in a change process.*

- *Power is effectiveness. Each one of us has more power in life than we know what to do with. How much of your own power do you use in being effective? What prevents you? Are your attitudes unconscious and defensive and used as excuses for the courage to take risks?*

- *The key to ineffectiveness is the childhood trauma and loss of power. Relive this experience now in enactment or active imagination and this time work it through so that you end up as effective in dealing with the attack on your own natural power.*

- *Commit yourself to certain life tasks which will demonstrate that you have changed the ineffectiveness pattern started in childhood.*

The measure of our effectiveness is the measure of power we are committed to using for realistic ends.

56 The Mother

Image: *The flowers are wilted in the vase.*

'A greater parent than my personal parents wanted me to be born.'

My mother seemed very much a woman, although she looked like Abraham Lincoln. She had character in her beautiful face. I think of her as the one in the family who almost always came up with a perspective on life.

She had considered herself a genius ever since her high school days when she passed all the exams without attending classes. She seemed an extreme introvert since she preferred to spend her time in the library reading. Having me, the unwanted child, must have been one of her greatest acts of extroversion. A more central parent than my personal parents wanted me to be born.

Memories of my mother are of a sick woman spending her time in bed drinking milk. My father would shop, go out into the world, meet people, and earn his living. My mother would stay at home painting, reading and writing poetry. Her goal was to be great, to achieve immortality through her writing. This also was my father's goal. Somehow they thought that will power plus talent would do the trick. Fame is ephemeral. It did not happen in their case. The recognition was quite minor.

I see a sickly woman afraid of life, with negative attitudes about how certain people were out to get you. Reality seemed harsh to her and she felt she had much to complain about. This has affected my own anima image in that I have been attracted to brilliant women who have problems making it in the world, creative women who are also sick with affliction.

My mother could talk for hours about the world, about literature, philosophy, art, music, politics, religion. So if my mother's focus was elsewhere, how then was my mother still a mother to me? It would be easy for me to resent her devotion to art and poetry, but my task is to look at events as they actually are so that there can be healing.

What then did my mother fulfil or not fulfil in my life at an archetypal level?

By looking at my anima, my inner feminine, I can see what my mother created of the feminine archetype for me. My anima seeks the

135

unusual and the exotic. It is concerned with spiritual things. It loves beauty. The women I have been drawn to, despite myself, have had a certain beauty, an inward look of the eyes as if dwelling much in the unconscious, and a tendency towards health problems. They have been dancers on the wheel of life, all of them. My anima also seeks women who can offer plenty of warmth and comforting. My mother didn't embody much of the nurturing side of the feminine archetype for me. She never hugged me or touched me except to shake hands when I came home on holiday.

My mother personified the frailty of the mind when it comes to the body. I couldn't quite tell her that her theories were crazy, but they were. Just before her death she told me she was on the verge of inventing an anti-gravity machine. Myself, I am a dancer, a martial artist of sorts, vigorous and alive with good health practices. I used to become nauseous when I was too thinking. This is an obvious reaction against my mother's mental nature.

Only in Jungian analysis did I realise I hated my mother. Thank God there were other women in the world. My mother was so powerful to me, I sometimes had to hide away in myself.

My own inner feminine has developed slowly over the years. My original defensive stance against my mother created tremendous inhibition and fear of the feminine. I had no flow to me in my younger adult years. At first I could not get angry or be directly sexual with a woman. That all changed through long Jungian analysis with women analysts, inner work, conscious changes in behaviour, and my relationships with women.

Our basic premise in working with childhood material is to realise that the parental archetypes within us were only partially created by the actual childhood parents. Our task as adults is to complete the archetype. Our compulsions, our needy child, will seek to fulfil those parts of the archetype left out in childhood. In my example I sought creative women who were also highly sexual since my mother seemed to have no sexual instincts that I could sense.

Mother, you were my inspiration and my difficulty. Now I see you with more peace in my heart because the feminine I have found is more than what you offered me. My own healing is within the archetype, not within what you gave me. You are still vivid in me but no longer the mother of my mystery.

The Work

- *Everyone's mother is somewhat different, but what feelings come up for you from the above description? What are the problems and what are the transformations?*

- *Describe your experience of your own mother with particular attention to what she did and did not bring out for you. What aspects of the feminine archetype did she show you and fulfil for you? What of the feminine was missing in your experience of her? How are you exploring new avenues of the feminine in relationships? In your inner life?*

- *What has been your own experience of mothering others? Are you identified with the archetype or related to it? Or both?*

- *Perhaps write a poem to The Mother, or paint her.*

To give you must let life in.

57 Early Loves

Image: *In the night a flash of light seems to lose itself in the moon.*

'When we're in the heat of love, we can do nothing, it seems, but go with it.'

When was the last time you felt consumed by love? Early passionate love lets us know, years before we can possibly integrate it, that a great mystery lies behind the love experience.

Love grows and consumes us, turns us around from whatever we were doing. When we're in the heat of love, we can do nothing, it seems, but go with it. Not to have fallen deeply in love is not to have experienced the passionate longing for ultimate unity in life. Maybe it did not happen for you in the childhood years, but only came your way as a young adult? Perhaps the full passion of love has not yet occurred to you? Who can predict when our moment is to arrive? Love comes when it comes, and our choice is to say yea or nay.

Sometimes dependency and the fear of moving out into the world are so powerful it takes the overwhelming power of love to move us to a new dimension. Whenever we are stuck in our ways, watch and see if love doesn't come along to pull us up and out into the next part of our journey.

Among my first experiences there was nothing so wonderful as being in love. The women I fell in love with are powerful for me in memory to this day. I so needed what they had, the enthusiasm, the passion, the flesh and dance of life. I was falling in love with life. My ego, my conscious side, can never quite be the guide into my future, because when love flies in new doors open to what I never knew I would experience in life.

How did we handle those early loves? Did we live them out without regrets, or did we feel frustrated when they did not last?

Gradually I learned to love life itself and to love expressing my true nature. Until I have found myself, I will seek to find love in another. And while I am finding myself, I am also a lover to those whose lot it is to share with me a common destiny.

Our ability to love is our ability to live life fully. The hesitations of the young years, the sexual play, the intense talking, the songs, the dance, are all forms of self expression for feeling the vital energy of life. The more we love the freer we are to love. There are no tragedies in love if we have loved fully. The sadness of love is the unacknowledged opportunities to love we let go by without action. To love is to give soul to what life brings. When you love, love fully, conquering fear by voluntary death of the old life and by giving birth to what must be. Love knows no boundaries where the soul is at work.

The Work

- *Write up your early love experiences whether they were realised or not. What feelings and dynamics did you experience?*

- *What have you learned over the years about love? Take a chance and write down a few things.*

- *What do you do to keep love in your life when you're not in love, or when you are not in a fulfilling love relationship? How can you feel just as creative about your life?*

- *Describe someone you have been in love with. Then translate their qualities into dynamics within yourself which you can live more fully in your life.*

- *Watch out for neurosis! It is the death of love. Find your early love trauma and transform it, or your ability to love will weaken. Neurosis makes us love those who are not right for us but who awaken our love wounds and the need for healing. How then do you use love for personal healing?*

Love lives where the heart is made free.

58 Sex

Image: *Bells in the night ringing.*

'. . . the yoni and lingam are one.'

In certain cultures children are allowed an almost uninhibited expression of sexuality. But for most of us our sexual feelings and expression have been coloured with moral, ethical and collective considerations. Our parents and our society may have visited upon us all sorts of dire forbodings about sex. We are not only left to carry the sexual energy given to each one of us in life, but we also have to drag around extra fears, traumas and attitudes about the sexuality.

If extra burdens have been added to our sexual lives then let us use sex to free us of those burdens. Fear of the negative hardly leads to being positive. Transforming the negative gives us hope. Note the following attitudes. These are hardly absolutes, but to the young person's mind what are merely attitudes seem like the last word of God visited on them by the parents.

> It is wrong for a child to masturbate. It is wrong to masturbate. It is wrong to masturbate in front of one's lover. It is wrong to go naked in public. It is wrong to have sex in public. It is wrong to have group sex. It is wrong to have sex when you should be working.

For contrast, note these 'adult' attitudes which are commonly accepted as positive. They show that while the collective attacks healthy sexuality, the serious issues of life go mostly unchallenged.

> It is all right to drink and get drunk in public. It is all right to make money out of another person. It is right to kill men, women and children who belong to the enemy. It is all right to lie to one's associates. It is right to lie sometimes to one's spouse. It is right to hate others on this earth.

These are all attitudes, not absolutes, but they show vividly the contrast between the forces for life and the forces for death at work in

140

the psyche of every person on this earth.

Back in childhood the sexual force began to grow in power while the adults sought to repress it in us, unless they were enlightened themselves about the act of love. Instead of letting sexual love remain pure in itself, the adults heaped excess baggage onto it. We return to childhood to see what that baggage was. We return to childhood to throw baggage over the nearest cliff. The worst you can do in life is pass on your baggage to the next generation. Let us find renewal and fulfilment in our sexuality, not trauma. Most adults have trauma and life-defeating attitudes about their sexuality which no amount of sexual exercises, sex manuals, or porno movies will overcome.

The healing way is not simply to get uninhibited by expressing sex, but to free oneself of the legacy of the past. What was it that your parents did to you that still hurts you today in regard to your sexuality? What sexual attitudes were you taught at any early age which act like knives against the fibre of your soul?

Sex is not only sex, it is mystery, the life force, renewal, and the source of our creativity and affection. Use it well in and out of relationship. Find wealth in the possibility for new unity daily. Do not die before the grave gets you. You are your own best lover. Be good to yourself and throw off the past. Yes, there is risk, but not disaster. Even the worst, if truly lived, has life.

The Work

- *Describe your earliest experience of sexuality. What negative attitudes may have been formulated in your experience and how might you transform them?*

- *What attitudes did you pick up in childhood about your own sexuality? What have been their effects on your life?*

- *Describe the beauty and grace in a childhood sex experience. How might you draw upon it today? What is sexuality for you now?*

- *For your sacred area you can make clay representations of the female and male genitalia, as was the ancient practice in most religions. In India they called the female opening the yoni and the male thruster the lingam. In divine ecstasy the yoni and lingam are one.*

Sex is God-play in the flesh.

141

59 Relatedness – Intimacy

Image: *A new configuration of stars in the sky.*

'. . . to be related I must yield my necessity to prevail.'

Relatedness is going towards others and opening to them as much of oneself as they can handle. Relatedness is also accepting and allowing others to approach and share with you some of their real selves. In relatedness we form bonds which enhance new life.

Non-relatedness is preserving my space against all challenges. Non-relatedness is my viewpoint prevailing in all situations, being right no matter what. Non-relatedness is not honouring the other person's perspective, is seeing the world through one's eyes alone. Even if I feel right in the situation, to be related I must yield my necessity to prevail.

Relationship is often not easy to achieve. From childhood onward we have defended ourselves against the universe and everyone around us. If I have a defensive personality, I am not capable of relatedness, and therefore relationship. If most of the time I feel more related to my objects than to those who would be close to me, I have little skill for relatedness.

Fear of intimacy also limits relationship. When we are about to become close to each other, one of us will throw in a conflict to split us apart. We want intimacy, yet we fear it. The way out? To come out of the protective castle into the real world where things hurt and things are wonderful.

Why do we hold onto our positions for so long? What a burden we give ourselves in having to defend our views about everything. If someone else has the better viewpoint in the situation, why not feel relieved? It takes so much energy always having to be right. All I want to do is live life richly, and the more you can contribute to our mutual journey, the better. Not having to be right also frees me to make a stronger contribution to our relationship.

In childhood most people have experienced parents who had to be right. By always being the ultimate authority parents neglect their job of being a supportive resource for their children. So as parents tried to control them the children tried to defend themselves. In adult life people relate to others the way they were related to as children.

Controlled children make controlling lovers. Controlling lovers create defensive and attacking lovers.

Greater suffering resides in having to defend oneself than in opening oneself to intimacy and life. Opening to life and intimacy will cause the weak and egocentric to leave, but in their place will come others of stronger fibre, not others with your point of view necessarily. There may be fewer potential friendships the more deeply the journey goes. But what is lost in number will increase in communion with yourself and with those who count. When you open doors to the heart, many will want to enter, but few will pay the price for such intimacy. We pay for intimacy by our willingness to change within the boundaries created by the union of honesty and love.

The Work

- *List the ways you became defensive in childhood rather than relational. What were you defending yourself against? Now list the ways you may still be defensive in adult life. What new ways of dealing with relatedness are there that you will commit yourself to trying out?*

- *List ways you have changed over the years to allow more and more intimacy. What were the causes of those changes?*

- *How might you have given up on relationship, not the need for relationship, but on your commitment to learning how to have fulfilling relationships? Search deeply within for those patterns and attitudes which may be defeating your willingness to be relational at a deep level. Challenge your intimates in terms of intimacy and relatedness.*

Honesty mates with caring to create intimacy.

60 Power

Image: *The child sits surrounded by peers.*

'The baby directs energy to get its needs met.'

What is power to a little child? Do the parents have all the power? What are the first uses of power by the child?

Power is energy. Or better yet, power is directed energy. The small child knows how helpless he or she is and must test the limits of reality to see where the power lies. Few parents can stand to have their children screaming and crying for long periods. Thus power comes into play. The baby directs energy to get his needs met.

What happens when the child begins growing up? Perhaps there is a constant struggle over power. It is not important nutritionally whether the child eats everything on the plate, but in many families it is important who wins the contest. Whose value is to be followed? Whose value wins out? The one with the greatest power to enforce it?

Certainly the most healthy family situation is one in which a balance of power is maintained most of the time. Did you grow up in a family in which your parents willingly allowed you to have some power? Did they yield their values, needs and wishes sometimes in order to go along with you? Of course they did, if you had loving, secure and conscious parents.

Or was it an ongoing struggle in the family to win power away from the parents? Or was the situation the other extreme in which your parents would yield to you on almost anything? If the parents are too yielding, then the child cannot find boundaries, the containers of power which we call reality.

There are those who would look out on the world and criticise its wrongs without ever creating power to correct them. And there are those who consider values to be ephemeral and arbitrary, and therefore focus mainly on increasing their power without much thought for how it is used.

Thus we have the power-seekers versus the idealists. Which side are you habitually on? Did you retreat as a child and remain critical of those around you? Was the world beneath you? Or did you think that in order not to get squashed you had to go for whatever power was available to you?

These questions are important because in order for us to be effective as adults in this life we must have power. The more power we have the more we will be able to change reality. But power also needs context in order to be fully effective. Power which focuses on itself will defeat itself. Yet power expressed within the natural principles of the universe can be extremely effective.

As adults, are we willing to go for power and use it to manifest true values in this reality? That is the real question. If we are not, we have probably been maimed in childhood in some great power struggle with the parents or family. Transformation is needed for the adult to use power, energy, money, influence, love, to create a renewed and revitalised life for oneself and others.

The Work

- *Pick two or three questions from the above text and work with them. Which questions would you like to avoid?*

- *Describe the power dynamics in your living situation when you were growing up. If there were stages, describe them.*

- *How, specifically, did you seize and withdraw from power?*

- *As an adult, what is your stance on power? How can you be more comfortable and effective with it?*

Power without consciousness destroys itself.
Consciousness without power lacks effectiveness.

61 The Family Neurosis

Image: *The wagon wheel lies broken.*

'I could redeem my life. I could feel again.'

In the family closet a neurosis lies hidden. Every family has a skeleton in the closet, the gaping wound closed over and hidden from public view, the family embarrassment.

Each generation passes on some form of the family neurosis to the next until someone chooses to make the anomaly conscious and transform it. Who wants children if we are going to plaster them with what our parents put over on us? Do we want to allow the maiming of our own child by our own hand?

My family on my father's side went through the pogroms of Russia at the turn of the century. The Cossacks ransacked, raped and killed the Jews. The terror created and intensified neurosis among the people. My father's generation of five children migrated to America with my grandparents. They never sought therapy. It was too new for them. They sought, instead, power, money, wealth, effectiveness and freedom. But what did they know about bringing up children to be healthy? Each of my own generation went into therapy. I myself have had fifteen years of it. I worked hard. I learned that I could redeem my life. I could feel again.

It must be strange for a small child to be born into someone's living myth, the adversaries, the coldness, the strange behaviour and wild views about reality.

This generation seeks therapy, understanding, and change so that their children are not burdened by problems other than their own. If not for oneself, we can change at least for our child's sake. We do not perceive yet what the new children will be like who have had a more conscious generation of parents. The weight of the generations is immense. Yet the greatest force on earth may be the healing power of consciousness, a power which can break decisively the chain of the family neurosis which has taken generations of denial to build and years of personal therapy to destroy and cleanse.

The Work

- *What were some of the things in your family which people tried to keep from you? What was your reaction to this? What sort of pattern is behind what was kept secret?*

- *How does the family neurosis show up in you? How are you a bit extreme in the same way? Or how are you an opposite to the family?*

- *How did your parents deal with the family neurosis? Did they reinforce it or fight it? What effect has this had on you?*

- *How would you say your wound or neurosis affects your children, or need to have or not to have children?*

- *What are you going to do to stop the family neurosis in your generation?*

We can defeat ourselves with our own blood.

62 The Friends We Had

Image: *The tree has lost its branches.*

'. . . seeing ever anew the rainbow in relationship and the broken bridges needing repair.'

When I was around ten I had a friend named Ron. I think he was taller than I and red headed like myself. Once a year we would have a great big fight, crying, screaming, and wrestling each other to the ground, trying to make the other give up. That was true friendship! He was my closest friend for many years. We would go off into the woods every afternoon after school, build forts, and dam up small streams. In the autumn, we would steal corn from the field and roast it on our outdoor, hidden fire.

When I went to military school at thirteen, that part of childhood ended. Somewhere in those early teen years I met a friend at a summer camp whose name was Israel. We climbed the mountain together and sat on the moss overlooking the valley of farmland, the neat fields of different colours, the future laid out before us. Yes, the future. Israel and I talked long about the future. We were close. We thought big thoughts. A sensitivity developed between us, an imperceptible aura of destiny. We had great ideas. We were nubile, not quite ready, but not yet encumbered by life. I saw Israel years later. He called me out of the blue. He had been to medical school and was professionally established. The glow was still there between us but we didn't quite hit it off. There was no recapturing childhood in an outer sense. My thoughts, my feelings, are of a different world long since gone down the path of long ago.

I shared the first mysteries of sex with Denise, Ron's sister. I was twelve and she eleven and we both found ourselves locked up in an isolation ward at the school infirmary with chicken pox. We made a house under the bed. I took off my pyjamas. She lifted up her shift. We were scared of the nurses and thrilled by our secret activity. My mother visited me and I felt so guilty about my friend. One day before I left that school, I was running through the fields in summertime and suddenly there was Denise with flowers in her hand. We looked at each other long and hard and then one of us ran away.

A friend is someone I can be real with. A friend is someone I have shared the deepest moments of life with. A friend is the witness in some essential part of my life. Come forward, my friend, and we will create the meaning of our lives. To be a friend is as much to be needed as to need. To be a friend is to practise love, compassion and anger, to delight where there is play, and to pound on the door when things have gone astray. A friend is laughter, love and pain, is the sudden recognition, seeing ever anew the rainbow in relationship and the broken bridges needing repair. I have chosen you, my friend. Is it your choice as well?

We let go of the past by taking the essence with us. My boyhood friends seemed vital to me. With them I glimpsed my own future and thought I was seeing theirs. Ah, the intense moments! It would take years and steady work to even come that close to the raw germ of life again!

The Work

- *Please write feelingly about your early childhood friendships or lack of them. What kind of person were you as based on your friendships? What kind of person were you attracted to in your friendships?*

- *Do you tend to have friends of the same sex or of the opposite sex? How do you explain your propensity? What might you do to balance things out?*

- *Review your present friendships using the following criteria. Is the friendship two-way and balanced? Do you get as much as you give? Do you give as much as you get? Is what you have in common central to the relationship? If not why are you relating? Are you being more and more open with your feelings, and is your friend opening up likewise? Are you keeping the friendship continuing past its dying point? Are you afraid if you let the friendship go there will not be another to take its place?*

We relate to others to relate to ourselves.

63 Abuse

Image: *Lightning strikes in the cave.*

'Every healing needs a wound.'

We were called into the main room of the cottage where thirty of we boys lived, aged ten to twelve, and told to remain silent by the older boys who supervised us. I looked over at my friend Ron. Our eyes met, but neither of us said a word. We both knew better than to make ourselves conspicuous at this time. An older, stronger boy looked us over and said one of the boys had had some money stolen and they wanted to find out who did it. Stealing was not uncommon in the charity school to which I had been confined since I was six. I myself never stole. I played the good boy, and would play the good boy again today. But I had at times tried to find the thief myself by hiding and observing suspicious children, forgetting for the moment that I was also a child. We knew of one boy who was a habitual thief but he was not taking the blame for this one – too bad for all of us.

The older boys had us lie on our backs and raise our legs off the floor and keep them there. With threats and insults they terrorised us until the pain seemed unbearable. Nobody confessed, so that we all had to endure the torture and fear. Then they took us one by one into a room and confronted us individually with shouts and pushes.

'Did you do it? Did you do it?' they shouted to each of us alone in that room with the upperclassmen. I played my most innocent self and so only got shouts and shoves. Another boy who had stolen in the past we found out later had been picked up and thrown against the radiator. The terror was extreme and this and many other incidents like this made me so repressed that finally I showed no feelings and kept an extremely even and subdued voice in everything, a voice which never changed until after many years of therapy. My insecurities burned me. My defence was to hide in invisibility. My rages were secret, even to myself.

Another time when I was older and now residing at a military school, the upperclassmen called certain of us out in the night to punish us for a wrong we had not done. I was made to pull down my undershorts and received many hard and stinging blows with a large wooden paddle. I wanted to throw the table over on the boy in charge, but my fear was greater than my anger. I was too inhibited to fight back, to take anger and run with it. I felt the situation as totally unfair. I felt impotent, insecure, lonely, helpless. I wanted revenge.

Abuse is the norm, is the great Adversary Archetype entering the child's life. Abuse comes by violence and by sexual misdeeds. We as children are victimised by those stronger than ourselves. It is our lot to be a victim to these great misuses of power. Better to learn in childhood that you are not all-powerful and that sometimes no one is there to help you in your time of need. As adults we cry out against and are hurt by the abuses we have suffered, but do we also accept them as natural? Am I to say that I should not have been severely terrorised as a boy? No, I cannot say that, I cannot go against reality. Beware the attitude which says that things should have been different. For fundamental to receiving the blows of adversity is also the recognition that no matter how difficult the circumstance we are also given the resources for self-healing and transformation.

The unrealistic attitude is to say that such-and-such should never happen to a child. It did happen and that is reality. To expect the good to triumph over evil, the hero to always win out over the adversary, is to cling to unrealistic attitudes and expectations. To accept adversity as natural is to become real to this life as it is.

Yes, of course I was beaten as a child. That is what certain people with power do to their victims. Yes, I was also sexually molested, but so what? Yes, I was forced to build an enormous defence system against the terror, but so what? What is crucial is that I also found the resources to transform the wounds done to me, to collapse the defence system and begin to live a healed and renewed life. Every healing needs a wound. Each of us will need to feel the Great Wound in childhood and try to defend against it. Then in adult life we can work it through and live differently. We can heal the wound of childhood by dissolving the defence system and living a transforming life in tune with the healing centre of the Self.

The Work

- *What was the form of abuse you went through in childhood? It may have been overt, either sexual or violent, or more hidden, even the wound of missing love and a fundamental understanding of who you were.*

- *Having described your childhood abuse experience, then describe the defence system you built to defend yourself against further abuse. Is this defence system still in operation today? How?*

151

- *Choose to let go of your defence system and move into a stance of dealing with anything which comes your way. If you are still a complainer or a rager, then you have not left your defensive personality yet. If you think there should not be evil in the world, then you still need work on your attitudes to make them realistic. Reality is healing. Idealism causes defeat and despair.*

- *Rewrite your early abuse trauma with a more healing outcome. This changes patterns deep inside. Let the full force of adversity rain down upon your childhood head, but this time deal with it more resiliently instead of repressing hurt or turning invisible.*

- *You have described what the trauma and defence pattern was in childhood. Now see how this pattern operates in your adult life. Then create alternate and healing ways for dealing with adversity today.*

What we flee from we become.

64　Egocentricity

Image: *A cracked egg lying at the edge of a table.*

'The way to get what you want is to not want it.'

Not one of us is always fun to be with. We each have our little foibles, our egocentricities which drive others up the wall.

We are egocentric when we act in ways to build up our own egos at the expense of others or of life. We are egocentric when we do not trust a larger process than ourselves, when we try to control, to get our own way in everything. We are egocentric when we act defensively and withdraw, or make ourselves unnecessarily available to others. We are also egocentric when we try to put everyone else's house in order but our own.

Fritz Kunkle, an American psychologist writing in the 1950's, describes four types of egocentricity. Two are developed by growing up in a harsh environment, and the other two result from growing up in a soft environment.

> The Star grows up in a soft environment and shows a marked extroversion. A Star wants the centre of the stage. The Clinging Vine grows up in a soft environment and shows a marked introversion. This type depends on others. The Bully grows up extroverted in a harsh environment. The Bully's response to difficulty is to try to dominate, no matter what the consequences. A Turtle grows up introverted in a harsh environment, with the tendency to withdraw in the face of adversity.

As described, these are essentially negative and defensive reactions to reality. The Star feels insecure if not at the centre of the stage and so tries to dominate with talent and energy, creating love. The Bully tries to dominate with power and aggression, creating fear. The Clinging Vine tries to dominate by neediness, creating concern. The Turtle tries to dominate by withdrawal, creating compulsion in others to break through.

The positive aspects of the above dispositions lie in their transformations. Behind each is a natural personality quality useful in life. There is a time to be creatively alone like a turtle, a time to be vulnerable like a clinging vine, a time to be expressive and 'out there' like a star, and a time to be assertive like a bully or strong person. The

153

transformation is in letting go of the defence system and living each of the dynamics appropriately as part of our own wholeness.

We look at our egocentricities to further study the nature of our defence systems produced in childhood, and to see their effects in adult life. How do each of us as adults tend to react to situations? If we do not know, ask our friends to type us. They know! To act defensively in adult life is usually not appropriate and prevents relationship.

In terms of early childhood dynamics the child develops ego by focusing on its own needs and wants. It gathers possessions. It chooses for itself more than for others. This is a necessary stage towards self-autonomy. Once a child has established his autonomy he will outgrow the need to focus so much energy on himself. If, however, this need for self-affirmation has been thwarted, the egocentric child will become an egocentric adult.

In the adult years to always choose first for oneself means that we will be offensive and even hurtful towards others. We will remain subjective and not objectively choose what is best for all in a given situation. We will antagonise others needlessly and have little in the way of fulfilling relationships. As adults we learn that we do not exist alone and are interdependent with others. We learn to choose for others as well as for ourselves. The cure of egocentricity is to put oneself in alignment with source energies greater than oneself, and in so doing we are being fed the vital stuff of life.

The Work

- *Make a list of your egocentricities and how you will transform them. Also make a list of a friend's egocentricities as you see them and share.*

- *What type are you? Star? Clinging Vine? Bully? Turtle? What was your dominant in childhood? Has it changed with the life transitions? What are its positive aspects?*

- *What would be the positive aspects of transforming your egocentricity?*

If we were not accepted as children we will not as adults accept others.

65 The Defence System

Image: *The castle walls are cracking.*

'I was far from the good person I hoped to be in order to get along in the world.'

My defence system developed in a harsh boarding school environment where I received little warmth, understanding or love. At times I played the bully. At times I withdrew. I repressed my feelings so much that my voice became even in tone so as not to betray emotion. If I showed anger or fear in childhood, there was a good possibility I would be beaten by one of the older boys. Being in a prison is how I think of my childhood schools. I became a warden to my own feelings. I would hurt inside but never show it. I would hide within my own secret thoughts.

Later in adult intimate relationships with women, my feelings and my anger would poke out. I had great fear of being rejected. And I played the bully. I thought that now at last in the warmth of adult sexuality I could get what I wanted. But in fear of not getting what I wanted, I would be demanding and try to make things happen. I was so defensive that even the smallest things would upset me. And since I was getting upset, others were upset with me as well. I was a difficult person to handle.

I was most defensive at a time when I thought most highly of myself. God knows I could not be wrong in any situation. I was not angry. I was not being unkind. The trouble existed in the other person. In therapy I chose to own my own shadow and not defend myself against it, but to accept and take it in, however embarrassed I felt. I was learning to recognise that being upset with someone means not that they are wrong, but that I have feelings and needs which are making an attempt to reveal themselves. Embarrassment is due to the ego-identification with the persona being suddenly shattered, throwing the person into their shadow.

My transformation came in letting my feelings out and becoming more direct in expressing myself and my needs. I realised I did not have to get what I wanted if I could express what I wanted. Not expressing my needs led to agony because I defeated myself in not asserting my wants and desires.

It is freeing to go from a defensive to an accepting personality. It

155

took years of confrontation and soul-searching, both in therapy and in relationships, to accept my egocentricity and my shadow. I was far from the good person I hoped to be to get along in the world. I found that the more vulnerable I became in a human way, the closer I got to people and the closer they got to me. My defensiveness had created distances which almost nobody could bridge. Now there was hope. I was willing to lie awash in a sea of blood and see if anyone would respond, even take care of me.

Although nobody came forward to care for me, my close associates and friends joined me with their own vulnerability. We became companions in the end. We worked side by side, each tending our own wounded, inner child. And that makes me laugh, and cry.

The defence system is a set of attitudes and behaviour we built up to repress feelings provoked by other people's aggression and even love. Instead of expressing our feelings and needs directly, we learn to manipulate situations and people in order to get some of our needs met. We act defensively. We live in anxiety and hide our vulnerability from ourselves and the world. We lose our energy and become rigidly locked into our defences, thus stifling the spontaneity of life and feeling. We rule our castle through our own worst egocentricities. We feel alienated and in danger of losing our humanity until at last we choose to leave the defensive personality, suffer the transformation, and live at last joyously open in grounded and exciting ways. We commit ourselves to consciously processing whatever comes up in life.

The Work

- *How would you describe, free flow, your own defence system?*

- *How might you begin to transform your defence system? What role does commitment play here? What would be some creative alternatives to having a defence system? Do we also accept our own defensiveness?*

- *What is the alternative to living defensively? Are you willing to let go, to risk, to live fully, dealing with everything as it comes along? If not, what is stopping you? Most likely it is your defence system which imprisons you as you attempt to shut out part of your world.*

We defend against that which we are unwilling or unable to process.

156

66 Ego

Image: *The ball is thrown through the centre of the circle.*

'No one can make our choices for us. The consequences we suffer alone.'

The birth from childhood into adulthood is the birth of the creative ego. To leave home is to leave behind letting others make decisions for you. You do want to go out in the world, don't you? You do want to make decisions for yourself, to sink or swim based on the actions you take? You are not afraid, are you, that you will make the wrong choice in something and have to pay for it yourself? Where are the parents in adult life to bail us out? If we mess up a major relationship, or are out of work, we can always come home, can't we? If we run out of money the parents will offer a loan or a gift, won't they?

Symptoms of a weak ego? Yes. We have spent all of childhood, unless we were wonderfully trained, relying on our parents and others in authority to suggest the right choices for us. Sometimes the only areas where we as young people could assert our own authority and choice-making power were in our hidden sex life or in the taking of drugs. Otherwise, the parents tried to control us, tried to tell us what to do, where to go to college, what to work at, what kind of friends we should have. This is, of course, terrible training in making choices. It is not the content of the decision making which is crucial but the process itself of choices and their consequences.

> To build a strong ego is to take responsibility for one's own choices and their consequences. The true adult chooses her or his own lovers. Pays her way in life. Does not follow a guru or any teacher who requires the giving up of choice-making power. Does not allow one's partner to have veto power over one's own choice-making. Does not rely on friends for advice on how to act in life. Does not remain ambivalent in the face of life choices needing to be made. Does not follow psychics, astrologers, therapists, and so forth, who tell one who to be with and what to choose in life.
>
> The strong adult relishes the tension between opposites as opportunities for conscious choice-making. Is decisive when necessary, or flowing when openness is required. Chooses as

157

quickly as the occasion demands. Actualises the potentials of life when ripe, through choice and action rather than waiting in fear and therefore missing the moments of greatest opportunity. Puts the ego in the service of deeper sources than ego so that choices may be well made and lead to fulfilment for those involved whenever possible.

Use the above characteristics for your own perspective on how you are doing. Prepare to graduate from childhood by making your own choices more and more in everything you do.

The great break-through in choice-making seems to occur in the late teenage years. It is then that most children realise that their parents no longer have superior wisdom and cannot make the right choices for others. Until this transition point, say around seventeen, the young adult sees problems as coming from 'out there'. The parents or the school, or whatever, want certain things. One is rewarded or blamed by others according to what one does.

The perspective changes as the young person realises that success will depend, not on others, but on what he or she chooses and does in life. 'Making the grade' becomes a choice, not luck or pressure from outside. The pressures are still there but the approach is now more through choice. I choose to learn, to study, to seek work, to have my own kind of friends, and so it goes.

The birth of the ego, of the independent choice-making function combined with a self-image of making it on one's own in the world, sets in. Some enter adulthood living in a self-determining, choiceful way. Others, who were never trained to choose, enter a sexual or religious relationship to maintain dependency, allowing others to take authority and make their choices for them. This hardly works in the long run. No one can make our choices for us. The consequences we suffer alone.

The Work

- *Write a short history of your own growth in choice-making and ego self-determination starting in childhood. What is the pattern there? What issues have you solved so far? What issues are left to work on?*

- *Describe yourself in terms of the chief creative ego characteristics of choice-making, self-determination, inner authority, independence, realistic image of oneself, ability to be effective and self-sustaining in life, and conscious awareness of yourself and others on a daily basis. Which of these characteristics did you achieve in childhood, and which are you achieving now in your adult life?*

The ego works on ego to become ego.

67 Healing

Image: *The serpent swallows its own tail.*

'We are sick in adult life because the wounds of childhood are crying out in us.'

When I was at my first boarding school I would get sick every year or so with vomiting and dizziness so that they would have to send me to the infirmary for a couple of days. This was a small hospital of twelve beds where you could stay overnight to be watched over by the young nurses. They would always make a fuss over me and give me ginger ale to cure my vomiting. I had to be sick to get some healing. The cold environment of boarding school was killing off any human warmth in me and I needed, at long intervals, to know that personal caring and love did exist in the world. My stay in the infirmary would then balance out my psyche and I could go back to the dorms to endure further suffering until I could finally escape from childhood into adult life.

We all have a need for healing, so this becomes one of our primary issues in life. Not only do we have minor illnesses throughout our lives but many of us achieve a major illness or two, some of which even kill us. It is quite possible that what motivates all illness, physical and mental, is that original wound from childhood which was not healed and transformed. We are sick in adult life because the wounds of childhood are crying out in us.

To heal is to bring resolution to a split, a malfunctioning in the psyche and in the body. When we are sick, certain organs are not working in their characteristic way. They are blocked, they are resisting the natural energy flow of life. Sometimes the old tissue or mental patterning must be cut out of the surround so that other functioning can continue. This is the radical step of eliminating the old and the useless. Healing is a protective act of eliminating the destructive.

The other face of healing is that which transforms. Again the pattern or organ is blocking energy, is refusing to be a part of the whole. We attempt to bring healing or resolution here by accepting the wounded part instead of resisting it. Healing brings the part back within the whole. A change in how energy is moved through the part occurs and the whole is itself transformed by including the part.

160

All trauma is originally a blow to the natural functioning of the organism. In reaction, the organism seeks to protect itself by building a defence system around the wound. We act defensively to prevent further blows from hurting us. In order to heal we must allow the defence system to be breached, the wound must be cut open and suctioned of its poisoning effect. As trauma is again exposed the wounded one goes through the agony again, but without defending against it this time. The full experience of being wounded is accepted as an energy to be dealt with rather than resisted. Resolution is then possible instead of defensiveness. The wound heals because it is brought within the whole. The whole functions again at full capacity because all of its parts are working together, none resisting or blocking the other.

This model applied to severe cases of trauma, such as child abuse, rape, accident and war atrocity, means that the sufferer would be guided through the experience emotionally with enactments, visualisation, dreamwork, and a feeling process. Energy is released from the repression and new life is possible. Being abused in childhood is not a life-long tragedy if worked with in depth. Everyone has adversity to deal with in some form. Staying angry, hurt and ineffective over one's wounds becomes indulgence at a certain point if transition is not made. We choose to experience the wound fully, then we choose to get out of the wound and live non-defensively but openly with a fresh creativity about life. I have seen this process work many times for myself and those I have done therapy with. When healing occurs we feel it as one of the great events of life.

The Work

- *Using the above description, take yourself through a healing process for some trauma of childhood still affecting you today.*

- *Describe how to deal with hurts in a non-defensive yet protective, integrative and whole way.*

Healing the wound wounds the healer.

68 The Inner Child

Image: *The old folks have climbed onto the merry-go-round.*

'There is only one holiday, the holiday of the heart!'

Within each adult we find a child, but when do we ever see that child? In severe illness with the collapse of the ego structure? In sexual intimacy? In old age when the adult persona is dying? Or in bouts of drunkenness and superficial party going?

Better to acknowledge the inner child when the need is there, the crying held in a friend's arms, the joyful teasing and playing out in the park, the running or walking for long miles in nature, the camping in the wilds. But also the angry arguments, the adult tantrums, the disappointments, the hurts unacknowledged, the lost possessions. All those ways the human adult species can become insecure and regress into the lost child.

If you ever doubted that you were fully an adult you had only to experience once again, and compulsively, the inner child ripening for action, breaking forth in all the moods of your being, the tension, the anxiety, the curiosity and enthusiasm about life.

We look to what the actual outer child can do well. Their sense of play, or spontaneity, of quick feelings, both positive and negative, their direct neediness, no beating around the bush, their quick learning on the physical and mental plane, their need for structure and encouragement. The inner child is that repository in us of all the unlived child aspects that never were well expressed in actual childhood. But the inner child is also what was well expressed and what we seem to have lost as adults.

And what is an adult? Serious above measure, determined to succeed in life, to be successful, always another goal in sight, always with too many things to do, maybe a compulsion towards order, and certainly a lust for objects, the measuring rods of needs fulfilled. The adult is a collector, a greedy person who gathers possessions, the little gifts he or she never received as children. The adult is an intimacy machine, a learner of ways from books, the sexual positions, how to satisfy a mate, what to say, how to fill the chequebook of love out properly, to be competent and judged a success. The adult wears clothes, textiles full of attitudes about the right way to do things in life. The adult is an ordered creature, a mature person who does not do that, whatever that is, because he or she does not want to be caught being childish.

Let's go on holiday then, let's go to the inner realms and meet the lost children, the kindergarten of the heart, there, and love again and be free. We need our inner child to break us from identifications with adult roles, to help us get back to that spontaneity and flexibility we might have had as children with new life bounding about.

Talk to your child, have a conversation with an inner aspect of your being, the vulnerable part, the part always new and ready for the next bit of life, curious, alive, scared, bad, or is it naughty? You will find renewal there, become less stiff, less serious about everything. Old age is as much the stiffening as it is the years piling in on each other. To balance the ageing process bring in with glory the child again, the spark of new life!

The Work

- *Having read the above passages aloud with friends, each person taking a turn with a paragraph then discuss it, or each person give their reaction immediately after reading their paragraph. Then, play the child.*

- *Get down on the floor, crawl around and over each other. Take turns holding each other. Play childrens games together, like board games, but break all the rules. You must get out of the adult game of winning!. Get out the chalks and paints and paint the child. Make music together, don't play the canned music from your stereo system. Get out the pots and pans and bang away. Use whatever is at hand. Talk baby talk with each other, be really silly. Take it from there, come up with your own tricks, even be naked together without being overtly sexual, get out the water hoses, the mud, the water paints, the wildness, the flowers, the wrestling, the massaging together. No sex! This is to release child feeling, not repressed feeling. What is being loosened up here is the adult persona so that you can be much more spontaneous in life and therefore feel new vitality and creativity. Being an adult all the time dulls the edge of things and makes machines of grown men and women. There is only one holiday, the holiday of the heart!*

- *Paint your inner child. Get out a large piece of paper and let the water colours or the chalks choose you. Let go and just let what comes come. Start with scrawls like the youngest of children would. Move your arms. If you feel negative reactions to what you are doing or producing, know that it is the adult you making judgements on the child you. You do not have to be good at anything now. Just be spontaneous. And what is spontaneity? It isn't anything you can pin down. Gradually move to another sheet of paper and draw your inner child. What is he or she doing? Sad faces? Happy faces? Do it! Don't evaluate what you are doing. Then, when done, share in an affirming way with others.*

- *Have a dialogue with your inner child, the child of the heart. Take paper and write out a dialogue without thinking. Ask your child how you can contact her or him and write whatever comes. Ask your inner child for new ways of acting in life, and write out whatever you hear in your heart-mind. Write until the energy goes. And let the feelings come up. Simply include them in what you are doing.*

The new child lives again when the old adult dies.

The Magical Child within the Garden

69 The Parental Archetypes

Image: *The chicken crosses the road.*

'Then as an adult you parent yourself.'

If you really want to be an adult you will have to solve your dependency problem. The way to do this is to develop a creative relationship with your inner parents, the parental archetypes, as well as with your inner children, the wounded and the wondrous child.

Until we have realised the parental archetypes inside, we project them outside and seek in others the parental functions we should really find within ourselves. You can spend years seeking the lost parent outside, years of frustration and misalignment, never finding what you so desperately seek. It is a lost cause. You cannot return to childhood to obtain all the nurturing and inspiration you feel you should have had from your own original parents, imperfect beings that they were.

You cannot get what you lacked then from them now. For the parents of childhood are not the parents of today. They have changed, if ever so little or so much, but inside you, you carry still the images and expectations from the parents of the past. This is what you must deal with if you are to truly graduate from childhood into adult life. It seems that most parents are not that equipped to bring up their own children. They have been miseducated by their parents, hit with the hand, abused sexually and violently, criticised for failing, given values to realise which were not their own. They have come imperfectly, even maimed, into the adult role of bringing up children. And you are the benefactor of all this, the legacy, the family neurosis. Is it any wonder you may hesitate or have hesitated in having children?

Then where does healing come from if not from the parents? It comes from resurrecting and healing the inner parents and the inner child. The parental archetype is a pattern within that can function to sustain you in life. Most people may be good at nurturing others but hardly able to nurture themselves. This is a symptom of not having the inner parental function of nurturing developed within. It works only when projected without. So much of what people call caring is really repressed agony. We love others, seeking to be loved ourselves.

166

If I love someone else they will love me in return, goes the attitude. But if you are loving another it is quite possible that you are loving them because they are wounded, and therefore incapable of loving you in return. The worst way to get love is to love someone else. Much better to act wounded and inadequate yourself so that someone will come along to parent you. Be strong and others will be weak. Be weak and others will be strong. This is the way the world works.

Is there no solution? None without consciousness of the process and how to transform it. When working consciously we have the parental functions available inside us. We can nurture another freely, not to receive nurturing in return but to express ourselves and to feel grounded by engaging in a healing process. And we can allow ourselves to be cared for by showing our vulnerability and even asking for what we feel we need. This of course takes a mature person relating to a mature person. So much relating fulfils the dependency syndrome, not the healthy syndrome. Dependency is manipulating the other person to meet your needs by acting more wounded than you are. I'll meet your needs if you meet my needs, goes the unwritten contract.

Return to Childhood. Solve the dependency issue. Develop the parental archetypes as functions within. Nurturing, Caring, Structuring, Directing, and so on. What the parents might naturally do with a child is also a potential for you to do with yourself. Then as an adult you parent yourself.

After the funeral of my father when I was thirty and he sixty-five I walked the streets of New York City that cold autumn, realising within myself that I was the only one left now. I no longer had a back-up person, someone to take care of me if things got overwhelming, although no one had come to my aid for years. My father was dead. My mother had died ten years earlier. I was to parent myself now, more lonely and more real.

The Work

- *Have a dialogue with each of your parents as inner parents. If they are living, call these dialogue parents the inner parents of childhood. These are not your outer parents now. Ask each parent what they represent for you, how you can find healing with their dynamics, and what you must do to parent yourself at this time in your life.*

- *If you have not already done so, start calling your outer parents by their real and human names. As long as you still call them 'mum' and 'dad' that will be as long as you project the parental functions outside and refuse to live the integrated life. Even though they oppose you, do it. For parental opposition or hurt is never to be acceded to. It is manipulation of the first order, the seat of many of your own problems, because still today they attempt to manipulate you into doing it their way, instead of affirming you as an individual realising your own potentiality. Give up the outer parents to contact the inner parents within.*

- *If you have a guru or some 'exalted being' you practically worship, look at this as a great big dose of projection. You have idealised the parent in hopes of having a more perfect childhood than you ever had first time around. To integrate, take back the projection, sever the outer relationship to get deeply in tune with the inner one. The guru will not like this, the guru wants followers, wants children who believe as he or she does. Why create spiritual dependency when you can have integration instead?*

- *List the qualities of the parental archetypes. Which ones did you experience in childhood with the original parents, and which have you sought out in adult parental projections onto gurus, teachers, spouses and so on?*

We come from without to go within to come out again.

70 First Sexual Experience– Traumatic

Image: *The rose has fallen, the petals scattered.*

'We do not redeem the dark side by avoiding it, but by encountering it fully.'

Our first sexual experiences colour the rest of our lives. The following life stories may be upsetting to you. Certain specifics can clash with your attitudes or evoke your shadow. You must deal with this. These cases are composits of what many people have gone through. Some experts suggest that one out of every three adults has been sexually abused. Let us have compassion on this wounding, both the wounded and the wounder. For the wounder surely has been wounded himself, and compulsively perpetuates the wound in an unconscious attempt at healing.

She was seventeen, attractive, but did not think well of herself. She considered herself ugly and definitely not popular, and so when the boy she knew asked her out and insisted on having his way with her she finally gave in. It was love of some sort, she reasoned, but it was also rape, and this cut through her heart. Now at thirty she is dealing with tremendous insecurities based on fear of being invaded.

He was around eight years old when an uncle sodomised his mouth. The man was ugly in action and in appearance. In spite of this, the boy grew up to be a man sensitive to love. He adopted a gay lifestyle, and was attracted to young men. They had beautiful bodies, but though sex was good the humiliation he secretly felt made him uneasy. In dream therapy he found how the original childhood trauma had coloured his adult years. He liked women but was drawn to men. He realised with a shock that he was trying to redeem the original ugly experience of violation by giving fellatio to beautiful young men. He found that he no longer had to do this because in therapy he went through the trauma of the rape, expressed his rage and hurt, and then on his own made the choice to include women in his intimate life.

Can you as reader take one more severe example of what happens to children when sexuality is traumatic?

She was seventeen and a virgin. She went out on a date with a boy from another town. He took her to his apartment to change his clothes and there forced himself sexually upon her. She submitted reluctantly, hardly knowing what to do. She was afraid of his violence. She was not in touch

169

with her own anger and felt helpless. Years later, after she sought help in therapy, she came to dream therapy because she was dreaming of dark males who would cause extreme fear in her without doing anything overt. She related to men but was afraid of them. Her dream therapy involved going through the trauma of the rape again in a two-hour guided re-entry. I played the male, playing all males in interacting with her. The rage, the anger, the sensitivity, the hurt came out. She said what she needed to say to her adversary this time around. She acknowledged how she had been robbed of a positive first sexual experience. She let it go, and I let go to the healing energy. Soon after this she met the right man for her, allowed herself to be open and vulnerable, they married, and she had her children and family at last.

We do not redeem the dark side by avoiding it, but by encountering it fully. The only redemption is in what can be different now. We cannot change the past but we can live differently in the future. Even a bad first sexual experience and its effects can be transformed. Some will be born to sex through adversity, and some through love. One is more painful. The other more joyful, if more innocent. The good as well as the bad can become an addiction, so ultimately it is what you do with sex that counts. Make your sexual life conscious, however it develops, and you will be more likely to integrate it into the rest of your life.

The Work

- *Write up or describe your first traumatic sexual experience with yourself or with another. What is the pattern emerging from this, and how has it affected the rest of your life, sexually and otherwise?*

- *Certain attitudes must have been generated by your early sexual experiences. What are these attitudes, and what are their effects on you? Which need changing? What can be more whole attitudes to replace the old ones?*

- *What are some ways you can work on releasing the trauma you may have around sex? To become sexual is to let go to and create with the life force. It's just that all sorts of other stuff gets in the way. What is in the way of your own sexuality?*

- *In a meditative state create for yourself a healing first sexual experience. Try to get into it at a feeling and image level. Perhaps masturbate with it also, or play-act it with a good lover.*

170

- *Find the child in you who has never grown up sexually and welcome him or her into the fold.*

The blade of reality cuts more deeply than love.

71 First Sexual Experience–Positive

Image: *A ring lies on a velvet cushion.*

'There are many ways to live but only one way to die.'

The first sexual experience is for some a fulfilling one, one in which the two people genuinely love each other to the extent they can. They learn together. One is not raped and the other is not the aggressor. Their opening to each other is gradual and mutual. They share in other ways besides sexually. And when they finally are without clothes together and freely expressing the caring, wild energy of mating, they are safe, they are in love, they are joyful in what life can be.

Such an experience will not last forever, or course. Kisses are sweeter than wine, as the song goes, but wine, the heaviness of life, may come in and end that which seemed so close to paradise.

The following is a positive example of the choice to love.

> She was all of eighteen, a warm and passionate young woman who nevertheless had not had sexual intercourse. She had dated several boys. Some had pushed for more. They were the wrong ones. They lacked subtlety, finesse. Then she met him. He was older than she by a few years. He was experienced, and yet not that experienced. He had not known a full relationship until he met her. She had deep feelings for him. They went through ups and downs, the splits due to parental pressure, the getting back together again in secret. They kissed passionately, talked all the time, went to the beach a lot, and to other places in nature, danced at the folk dances.
>
> One day they were finally naked together. She almost felt herself ready to have him, her first man. He hesitated. They did other loving things. He wasn't sure why, but he was scared. Perhaps he didn't want her to open up to other men after him? He knew he did not want to lose her.
>
> Then in early spring she came over in the afternoon to his house when his roommates were away at work and school. The rain fell gently with a moist fragrance. The morning glories outside his windows looked lush in their purples and pinks. He had resolved in his own mind what he would do. He was making a commitment. She had her own key to the house and let herself in. He was under the covers in bed in his back room. She knelt by his side and kissed him, and he invited her to take off her clothes and climb into bed with him. They felt warm and cosy together, warm with caring,

joy, the quiet spring afternoon, warm with love passion as they kissed and rubbed together. She thought that he was stimulating her like so many times before, arousing her to the warm releases that made them both sing inside. His mind was resolved as he slowly with each stroke penetrated her. To be fully inside for the first time seemed so special as he felt himself deep within the depths of her loving being.

He told her he was in all the way and she woke from her passion in surprise and realised that yes, they were completely connected, yes, they were one, they were intimate and excited with each other. The fires of their mutual life which had so long been smouldering now took off, lifting them both beyond themselves into the realms of ecstatic being, the great passion whose fruit was love.

It was her first time. Now the evening was arriving and the natural light took on a softer glow. He saw her there all naked in the mirror looking at herself, tears rolling down her cheeks. He held her as she let go, an infinite sadness, a new opening to life. For by this birth their death would also come. He had been offered one of the great gifts of his life-time, and he had given her with caring her first full experience of love, a safe experience, a feeling experience, a letting go to life. She looked so dusky there in the mirror against his lighter skin. Their bodies and their being revealed in the mirror on the wall of time.

He made up a poem for her and for their love in front of the mirror before they dressed, before they moved on to eat, to talk, to live. She looked to see how she was now different after the full love-making. She would later walk around on campus with a new secret. She had a lover, a man in her, a new step in life as a full woman. The love they kindled finally led to marriage, to more love, to divorce, to new love, to children, to divorce, to new life. The wheel of death and birth moves always forward. Adversity follows fortune, as misfortune is the prelude to new life.

This life episode is used to show what a major transition can be like if it is freely chosen at the right time in the right place. But simply having a positive experience of transition did not make life any easier. In some ways the positive experience is less a preparation for life than the negative one.

We who journey with wholeness as a commitment learn to take both the positive and the negative in equal stride. The good things need as much healing as the bad. But who would dare to take the beautiful experiences away from us? To experience beauty is to experience wholeness. We know how far we have fallen if, once having found life, we cannot choose it passionately over and over again, even in the midst of severe adversity.

Return to childhood then, to those beginnings and transitions wherein we first learned to drink of life, and find there what it is to live out the pattern, to desire fullness instead of decrease, to desire wholeness instead of dwelling in splits and one-sidedness, to choose life in the wonder and agony with which it comes to us.

The Work

- *Write up your own experience of sexual transition. It can be with another or alone, late or early. It was a significant moment of your life. Relate to it now for its essence.*

- *To heal a negative first sexual experience, face the trauma and the defence system it produced in you. Then go on to recreate in your own sacred imagination what would be the most healing first sexual experience you could have had. This resets the archetypes within you, freeing you to express more fully the life force in sex and other activities.*

- *How have you lived up to the potential of your first positive sexual experience? What kind of person are you as seen from your early experiences, and how are you actualising those dynamics today? If you feel you have regressed sexually, choose life!*

Life yields to time and time to essence and essence to love.

72 The Animus

Image: *The hat sits on the table.*

'The goal of all projection is integration . . .'

The animus is the masculine energy within a woman. In the love experience we project our dominant's opposite onto the other sex, or onto the opposite within the same sex. A woman generally projects her animus onto a man or onto the animus of another woman. The natural purpose of this type of projection is to get us into relationship so that we may experience and then integrate the projections back within ourselves.

Thus in childhood the young daughter plays out and embodies her father's anima, and he in turn becomes the recipient of his daughter's animus projection. She projects the masculine, and he projects the feminine.

In projection we first see out there what is inside us. It is easier, and usually far more dynamic, to see the strength and decisiveness of the masculine as being in the father rather than being within oneself, especially if the girl is being brought up in frills and lace. If a woman is being educated to identify with the feminine only, the strength of her projected masculine will be correspondingly stronger.

If, however, father is weak in masculine and mother strong in it, then daughter may have a more developed masculine herself. She identifies with her mother and acts strongly. The daughter will react to a weak and passive mother by going against her own feminine and over-developing her masculine side. As an adult she will seek men weaker than herself so that she may never become weak and pathetic like her mother has become.

In the early years the projections need to be lived out. Thus we have the first early love experiences, the crushes on the same sex or opposite sex teachers and onto various friends. You can get a good idea of what your animus was, and perhaps still is, by looking at the qualities of the receivers of your animus projection.

For some young women, their first love is a horse, the magnificent and noble animal whom they learn to tame in order to run freely with. Relating to an actual man comes later. We all know the story of the sophisticated young lady whose first sexual experience was with

175

the groom in the hay of the stable on a rainy afternoon. They rutted like the animals they were because the archetypes, the great energies, were at work.

The young man in childhood also tries to embody the masculine by identifying with it. How he dresses, his behaviour, his accomplishments and swagger, are the young man's attempt to identify with and live out his masculine to attract the opposite sex.

The goal of all projection is integration, whether we achieve it or not. The animus is a wonderful dynamic in a woman, for it gives an edge to her natural feminine, a bite, a reservoir or power which says that she can be competent and decisive in her own right, and achieve her purpose in life without benefit of a man's living it for her.

The Work

- *Who did you project your animus onto as a young woman? What were the qualities projected? As a woman, how did your mother's animus affect you? How did your animus reflect your father's? How did your animus affect your mother? As a young woman, how did your animus affect the men your own age? How did they influence your animus? As a woman today, how do you relate to your own animus? How do other women or men relate to it?*

- *As a young man, how did your mother affect your ability to relate to the woman's animus? How did your father influence this same ability? Where are you today in terms of your ability to relate to a woman's animus? How do you do it? What do you do?*

We first project what we need to become.

73 Father

Image: *Light breaks through the clouds.*

'Someone has to demonstrate to the child that the world can be effectively handled.'

My father was never in heaven, but when on earth, and all the time I knew him, he was special to me. Not only would he cook my meals and take me out when I came home on vacation, but he also was famous, which meant I had some admiration from the other boys. Only they interpreted it as being rich, and I was actually as poor as Ben Franklin's church mouse.

I looked up to my father as a boy, not only because he was taller than me, but because he was always telling me what to do. He seemed to know how the world worked. He would try and help me get along with people and deal with what was apparently going to be a pretty harsh reality when I grew up. In fact, from his view of things, I sometimes wondered if I should grow up. Maybe I wouldn't make it out there? He saw the world as beset with adversarial forces you had to fight against.

I remember one time my mother telling me how my father fell down the elevator shaft. Of course, I could hardly keep from laughing because I always thought my father was invincible. Apparently, in the dark he had assumed the elevator was on his floor when it was not, and he had stepped off into space. He had to walk on crutches for a while. My mother always said father had courage because he didn't complain about the big things.

Another time both of them were walking home past the drunks and the seamen of lower Manhattan, and on the dark narrow street where they lived, a husky drunk tried to drag my mother off by the hair. Oscar pulled in the opposite direction and together they got themselves into their building safely.

When I think of my father, I think of him as someone who could go out into the world with all its terrors and deal with things and be successful. He must have been arrogant as well. When a boy on a sled knocked him down from behind in the snow, I laughed. My father didn't like it at all. He said I shouldn't laugh at things like that. But I couldn't help myself. I laughed without end, so great was the humour of life suddenly coming in and momentarily tearing him out of his

177

dignified place in the world. It had been done to me by my father and now a little boy had turned the tables.

Within the father archetype reside the primary qualities of relating to the world, acting decisively, doing what is necessary to earn a good living, being effective, being directed towards realisable goals, and having a steady strength. Not all fathers achieve the potential of the role. Many women also have to embody these qualities for their children, especially in a changing world where the roles hardly hold any more. The roles change but the functions remain. Someone has to demonstrate to the child that the world can be effectively handled.

The Work

- *Write a description of your own father, including whatever experiences and characteristics come into mind. Then draw out the significance of your picture. What were the values he embodied?*

- *Write a description of the ideal father, or the fully rounded father. How much did you have or not have? How does this show up today? How has your experience of your father affected your relations with men?*

- *For the woman, which men in your life have been like your father, or totally different from your father? How is this significant for you?*

- *How has your personal experience of father affected your concept of God as father?*

- *How successful are you in the world? How can you tell?*

Success is knowing the laws of reality and using them effectively.

74 Dating

Image: *The fingers touch while on the grass rests a butterfly.*

'We test ourselves in life.'

In dating we learn to develop friendships, we learn to play together, to kiss, to caress, to make love, to argue, to help each other out, to be intimate. We all seem to want a daily companion by our side and so we must get out there in the real world and keep meeting people until the right one clicks. In our teenage years we became concerned about our bodies, how we looked, and our social skills. We wanted to be liked. We wanted to have friends. We were afraid of rejection, often having already suffered a severe rejection within our original family. The hormones urged us out. The fears kept us in.

In this contemporary society where major relationships may change every few years, the phenomena of dating still has relevance. Imagine your major relationship has ended and you have been out of circulation for a while. What do you do? Where are the people who would make good companions? And how do you go about attracting and keeping the right one? How many prospects do you have to date and sleep with until you find the match for you? Generally expect to date ten people to find the next right one for you. Why this number? It means keep dating until the right one meshes with you. Don't try and make the first relationship be the ultimate one.

It cannot be hard to imagine what it must be like to enter the dating arena for the first time. How is it done? How do I handle my emotions, as well as relate to the other person's? What will make me attractive and interesting? What will hold the relationship together? Should it be held together?

Our purpose is to explore those first times to understand them more clearly and accept them so we can evaluate our present performance in the relationship game.

Entering the dating arena we replace innocence with the ability to get involved and uninvolved in relationships. We test our effectiveness in our ability to bring a significant someone into our orbit to love. We test ourselves in life. We use all our resources, our psychological awareness and our ability to love – remembering once again that in loving our contemporaries we are still working through childhood problems first projected onto our parents and then onto significant others.

Everyone can find a mate. It is not based on how naturally beautiful you are. A beautiful and vital personality can be developed which will make even your physical appearance attractive. If you are not seeking or bringing to you good possibilities for a relationship check out whether your 'standards' are too high, thus denying opportunities there in reality. And check out also whether you are 'lovable.' Do you love to love, do you love life, and ultimately, do you love yourself? No one loves a loser. Everyone loves someone who loves. To be loved, love!

The Work

- *What does the above exposition seem to be saying to you? Make a list of questions or issues raised by the material in relation to your dating experience.*

- *As a teenager what were the questions you asked yourself about dating? What was your focus?*

- *What was your dating or relating pattern as a teenager and young adult? What is your pattern today? What is the difference or transformation?*

- *How much of your inner thoughts do you share with your partner? Why? What is the value in sharing and not sharing?*

- *What is the secret to successful dating or relating?*

- *If you are in a long term relationship, do you use your relationship as a safe place to hide, avoiding interactions of the sexes? Or do you still live all your interactions fully?*

- *What do you think your partner is doing with his or her secret life regarding the masculine and feminine of the sexes? It does not have to be overt. Whatever happens in fantasy and the heart is also real.*

- *How realistic are you about the relations between the sexes? What are the lessons in this complicated interplay?*

Wear your troubles on the outside and no one will see your heart.

75 Incest

Image: *The flower is lost in the whirlpool.*

'Healing childhood is a large order served at the restaurant of the gods.'

It may seem shocking, but it is a psychological fact that most people in their adult life create psychological incest. We marry our parents. We seek out our parents in adult lovers in an attempt to heal the childhood wound, the wound that says we were hurt by a cold and critical parent, or an absent parent, perhaps an alcoholic or abusive parent. We seek to mate with someone who fits the parental description in an attempt this time to transform the 'parental personality' through love.

It never works. We receive some healing in the nurturing which sex and companionship bring, but we do not solve the parental problem deep in our psyche. It is only within the myth of childhood that you can heal the wounded child by healing the parental archetypes. We must work on our complexes directly and not expect our friends and lovers to heal us.

In this sense almost all couples need relationship counselling to learn to communicate and resolve openly, to see what is being projected onto each other which really belongs to the myth of childhood.

We can get over psychological incest, but it may take years. Recognise that you are mating with a parent, someone you want to take care of you, and you will be more cautious and sensitive to the issues. Being unconscious has its advantages. Better not to know whom you are really mating with. You might turn off. In point of fact many couples do turn off to each other sexually and affectionately. Incest goes against nature and they begin to realise that they do not want to sleep with their parents. They want a real companion who does not remind them of the childhood mess. They want to mate with someone who does not try to make them a child.

Even though physical incest seems more horrible than psychological incest, it can be worked with as well. Healing will take place if the parties involved go through dealing with the experience without repressing. Physical incest is unhealthy primarily because it bonds the person to the parent in archetypal ways which are regressive and invasive. Sexual bonding with parents limits the possibility of bonding with one's contemporaries. Many parents may also practise physical incest without actually having overt sex with their children. Certain physical caresses may seem borderline, but it is the seductiveness of the parents which is most damaging. If the parent attempts to keep the teenager bonded to him or her, this borders on physical and psychological incest. The youth needs to break away and find mates outside the family. The original childhood family should no longer come first.

Let your children go. And children, free yourself. For the world is a much bigger place than your family arena can ever be. The world family needs you more than your childhood family has the right to demand or ask for.

Parents who practise open and non-seductive bonding with their children are giving them experiences of human warmth which will enable them to bond freely with others. The love you give your children must be a gift, not an obligation, so they can give it to others. Love is an outward spiral, not an inverted loop ending in an impossible knot.

The Work

- *How have you psychologically slept with your mother or father in your life? What were the good points and the awful feelings associated with the experience? How have you begun to experience change in this pattern?*

- *What commitment will you make to break the 'mating with parents' syndrome and find your true mate, the one who is like you rather than like your parents?*

When we are not free to bond we cannot bond to get free.

76 Work

Image: *The rope has caught the snake's head.*

'Do I bring defeat or accomplishment into my life?'

In graduating from high school we were ready to go out into the adult world and work, earn a living, practise our survival skills. Perhaps we married instead, or went to college, or travelled. But eventually work would come upon us. We would have to create money in order to live. We would have to find a structure for our lives.

Who likes to work? Retirement is looked forward to by many in this culture as the time when the person can do what he or she wants. But the young must put in their toil and sweat, they must take the best part of the day to labour. The young do the routine labour of the civilisation, along with older people who have lost or never developed their full usefulness.

Many slot themselves into a job where they can advance to more responsibility and greater earning power, but the best goal of the working life is to know reality in such a way that you make your work your most individual and creative endeavour. You make money and contribute to society doing what you are best at doing.

To get to the arena of the creative often takes an apprenticeship in routine study and tasks which undergird so much of the advanced work of life. To be the best you must go through the worst. How we were trained in the routine jobs of childhood either helps or hinders us from choosing what is necessary to move ahead in adult life. Pray that your family made you do what you did not want to do as a child so that you may be equipped for the reality of mature life.

Retirement is often the refuge of the burned out who have chosen to fit themselves into a work system which was not fulfilling. You know that you have found your own destined and creative work if you never retire from it as long as you are able to be effective. Retired people can return to the creative part of childhood and start new careers which express more their talent and passion. The choice is not to go to rest but to new activity. This will keep one passionate as long as one lives.

Most of us do not want a boring job. We want to work in an area where we can express who we are, our values, abilities and passion for life. We like to believe in what we are doing as beneficial to the world. We like to feel that if we put a lot of creative effort into what we do, it will make our job more lasting.

We may also want to make good money so that we can do things beyond merely surviving. We may want to climb the ranks, to move up the ladder according to our efforts and abilities. We may be reaching for more and more responsive situations for our drive.

But so much comes down to attitude and self-image. Do I work for myself, or for others? Am I willing to do the disciplined routine work as well as the creative and new? Is my goal money or satisfaction in The Work?

And on the metaphysical level, am I open to obtaining the prosperity and fulfilment which is there for me in life? Do I complain about my lot, or do I make choices which change things and manifest new possibilities?

The major defeat takes place within our own head. Reality has both the potential for destruction and for fullness. Which I go for depends on my attitude and self-image. A negative self-image is poverty itself. It is so easy to enjoy the results of one's labour rather than complain about what one has not got. Do I bring defeat or accomplishment into my life?

The big challenge in graduating from childhood is to go to work, to work at what you are meant to do in life, to risk and not play it too safe within the nest. If your motivation is security you will forever fail at dealing with fear, you will miss opportunities, and no amount of money will make you feel safe or happy. To work at risk is to live at the edge where the action is, to go for the new opportunity and actualise yourself in a changing world.

The Work

- *Describe your childhood attitudes and practices regarding work. Were you successful and praised, or criticised and ignored? What pattern and attitudes were created for you towards work and productive fulfilment? Write out a plan to change this now, today, and forever. Seek whatever help is available to change yourself so that you can accomplish fulfilment in work.*

- *Even if you are secure in a job and in your life's work, there may be areas of new fullness for you. What then are your job-related values and attitudes? What stands in the way of maximising your potential?*

184

• *What exactly is work for you?*

Success is doing only what you are meant to be doing.

77　The Persona

Image: *The painter's canvas is blank.*

'But nothing much gets revealed when we reveal the obvious.'

Everyone needs a persona to get along in the world. Quite simply, we do not walk naked in most public places. Our persona will prevent us from doing such a thing. Shame and embarrassment are feelings peculiar to an ego identified with the persona, the good and safe side of the personality. We are not our personas, except when we identify with them, which is often.

But even if we walked around naked not much would get revealed. The next barrier would still remain, the next inhibition to absolute freedom would still exist. People can see all of us as they did when we were babies and yet we will remain hidden from them if we choose to hide behind the mask of who we present to the world.

As children we are first groomed by our parents, then we start grooming ourselves, making our body look presentable, neat, even beautiful according to collective values. Along with the grooming we are taught what to say and not to say to others. We are being educated in correct speech and correct behaviour. We identify with the good parts and seek to carefully hide the bad. What attitudes about what is right do we still live out as adults? What is the way to dress, and for whom? What is the appropriate way to act in various situations?

Who is there who has not in their childhood stolen something from someone else? If you have not, why not? Chances are the completely above-board personality is a rigid one. If you identify with your persona, you will create just as big a shadow which those close to you will see and you yourself will be blind to.

The persona itself needs to be related to rather than identified with. My persona is the various roles I play out in the world in order to be effective in it. I can embody certain collective values and stay within the limits of the current trends. I can play the game. We get paid for our personas. I must look and act effective in what I do so that others will value and pay me for my services.

We develop and complete the persona for each stage of life. The first years of my life I played the good child or the bad child. One role

186

got love and the other got blame and deprecation. I soon learned that in order to receive love and caring I had to be good. Then as I left childhood I adopted the behaviour and role models of my contemporaries. I made my persona appropriate to my age and culture. I became effective in the world.

The Work

- *Is your persona appropriate to your present stage in life? If not, what will you do about it? Evaluate whether you have been affecting a persona beyond your years.*

- *What was your persona like as a teenager? How is it different now?*

- *What is my positive image of myself? What is the image others have of me? How do the two images compare?*

- *How would I like to be seen in the world?*

To be seen, put on a mask.

78 The Shadow

Image: *The tree falls over on the giraffe eating from its branches.*

'The new path is one of increasing emotional honesty . . .'

I remember visiting my parents as a child and wondering about their hidden lives. I somehow knew that my mother only revealed certain things about herself and my father. How I longed to know all about their lives, but, as I was reminded, there were certain things you just didn't talk about.

> When I opened the large black trunk after my father's death I found certain objects from my mother's life which I know my father would never have told me about. I hesitate even now to describe some of what was in that trunk, so frail at times seems the human condition.
>
> I found it somewhat pathetic to find my mother's typewriter with a page still in the paper roller where she had typed over and over again,
>
> > I am a genius
> > I am a genius
> > I am a genius
>
> When alive this crazy part of her must have been trying to evoke a genius quality to produce great poetry. It was an act not to be revealed to anybody.
>
> Also in that trunk I found some paper tissue with dried, yellow, sputum, obviously coughed up from my mother's throat as she lay dying. Such was the shock of her going that my father in his desperation tried to preserve anything he could. He had labelled this bit of uselessness,
>
> 'The sputum of the late poet, Gene Derwood.'

I am disclosing something meant to be kept hidden. I am disclosing my parents' shadow. People do strange things when their shadow pops out. Normally my father seemed as sane and rational as anyone, but the shock of his grief triggered his shadow, producing an extreme act of intense feelings. Normally my father was a tight, self-contained man with a good wit. This was his persona. He did not have much feeling expression. Feeling was in his shadow, and so it came out in unusual ways.

All of us have a shadow, the repository of the repressed and unlived life. In it we place what others do not like about us and what we also dislike in ourselves. We build our persona, the acceptable side, by repressing the unacceptable. I grew up believing I was a pacifist. I felt contempt for violent people. In therapy I learned to my chagrin that I could be aggressive and violent, that I had a lot of anger inside. I had grown up building a persona of being a nice child, to escape punishment. In doing so I had repressed my shadow, my dark, violent side, and had projected it onto others.

In adult intimate life our shadows come out in full swing to plague our partners. You may love each other dearly, but if your shadows are incompatible, you will not be able to live together without repressing.

We need to redeem our shadows and find appropriate ways of expression for them. It is true that we cannot simply vent negativity all over the place. We can learn in our adult intimate relationships how to express rather than repress the creative energy of the shadow. The new path is one of increasing emotional honesty in which we accept more of ourselves, including the shadow, and find ways of expressing these vital forces of life.

The Work

- *Describe what you know of your parents' shadows and the behaviour they used to repress their shadows. Then see how their shadow pattern affects you. What was unacceptable in your family? What parts of yourself do you feel were repressed or neglected? Which of these parts have stayed repressed in you? And what can you do about their expression now?*

- *Choose to discuss with your intimate partner how the shadow pops out or needs expression. Design play forms for expressing each others shadow. This can be in sexuality, play fighting, fantasy enactments, role playing.*

- *Bring up ways to contain, but not repress, your shadow. Containment is the conscious choice to set boundaries for how energy gets expressed.*

The ego has forgotten what the shadow knows.

79 Healing the Father Relationship

Image: *The hammer strikes the nail home.*

'The father goes for the value and never looks back!'

What is all this fuss about forgiving your parents? Sure, they did the best they could, but their best was sometimes not good enough. Fair enough. Then why forgive them for making life difficult? To try and reconcile with the actual parents is often a frustrating experience. Many factors mitigate against a successful conclusion.

To begin with, our parents of today are not the parents of childhood. Our parents of childhood are now archetypal memories and patterns within our psyches. It may not help that much to forgive a person, your parent, who is not today your parent of fact since you are no longer a child. Or are you still acting the child when you are with them? Then indeed, their influence on you goes deep and acts as a restraint on your full maturity.

Second, the parents of today may not, because of their personalities, be capable of that much change in relation to you. Asking those old parents of today to heal your childhood for you by becoming the parents you always needed but never had may be asking too much of them. If you put more on them than they can handle you will disappoint yourself and them. We solve our childhood problems through inner experience, not outer.

Third, your parent or parents may no longer be living, and then what do you do? You have no relationship to heal. With their death the relationship is forever broken. Or is it? Is there another way?

Fourth, sometimes through confronting the actual parents of today shifts in the relationship can occur which are felt as quite healing. Perhaps they are. It is healing to get to the place where you and your parent can discuss anything honestly and with caring, without either one of you pulling a power play or manipulation. Can you achieve this? Don't hang all your hopes on it. Be ready if the opportunity presents itself. Yet life is short and sweet. There are other, usually more effective, ways to heal childhood.

The key to dealing with left-over parental relationships from childhood is to get to the inner factors. Just what is it that the parent

190

still represents for you as an adult? What needs transforming there? How can it be done?

The Dream Father

My father died in 1964 when I was thirty and he was sixty-five. I had visited him in New York for about a week a few months before his death by throat cancer. We had great difficulty in communicating. He said little even though he took me and my wife to dinner. He never shared anything intimate about himself, or asked me about my personal concerns. I was repressed myself, the result of a long sojourn in boarding school. So we failed to communicate, and then months later he died and I returned to New York for the funeral. I felt grief, but what is grief but the mourning of the lost or unlived life? It seemed as if I was sad for him losing his life, but I was really sad because I had lost the chance to have a meaningful relationship with him and heal. We look after ourselves. Parents are important to children primarily because they sometimes help children to grow. I needed my dad, and I didn't know why.

A dramatic development happened. Over the next fifteen years I had the most healing relationship with my father that I had ever had. The lost life was found, experienced, and lived. I achieved healing of the father-son relationship.

It all occurred in a series of dreams during my long Jungian analysis and after. First the dream father-son relationship was rather cold. Then as I got in touch with my true feelings for my father and expressed them in therapy and journalwork the father dreams began to change. I visited his old apartment many times in the dream state. Almost each time the apartment was larger, more airy, with the windows bigger and the vista more expansive. In one dream I received from him a set of his books which he had written and had published during his lifetime. He was a well known poetry authologist. This was wonderful for me. He was actually giving me presents. Yes, I had received his books from him while he was still alive, but it always seemed that he was proud of himself. He gave his books away as an affirmation of himself, not as affirmation of another. I felt so inadequate when I was with him, even though I already knew I had a good mind. But in the dream state these gifts from him felt as if they were for me and my heritage. In therapy I had been working through the rage to a place where I could accept him for what he was and face that I also had a heritage from him genetically and relationally. I had to accept that I was like my father in significant ways. That was hard.

Then in another important dream he gave me a large book. It was

191

not his book but my book. It was the book of my life, unopened as yet, and certainly with blank pages. What a gift! More this time than the heritage. This was my own destiny, the blessing passed on from one generation to the next.

I had many dreams with my father in them over the following years, and in the outer I became much more effective in my work as a writer and teacher. The father represents relation to the world, success in the world, dealing with the world and becoming effective in it. This was happening through my work and development. I was integrating the father archetype within me and no longer resisting it.

The Amazing Dream

And then finally came an amazing dream. I was holding my father in my arms as he was visibly growing very old and dying. Crying the whole time I held him, small and wizzen, frail, without his enormous power any more to dominate and destroy me. I felt such compassion and tears. I felt I had come to know my father then, after I ceased resisting him. He was around 96 years old when he died in my arms that dream night. Crying away, I was amazed. I woke shaken and alive. I had let my father go. I knew now that I would not have many more dreams of him. I was truly losing my parents, and how appropriate that was. I seldom dreamed of my mother either. For once we have integrated the parents, and live the parental functions ourselves, we do not need to dream them.

Yes, I worked through acceptance and healing with my parent. The dreamworld gave a greater flexibility and healing than would have been possible in the outer if my father had lived on. But then maybe he needed to die so that I could achieve my own purpose? Certainly unintegrated I was still unconsciously dominated by parental energy and therefore in rebellion against it and unable to fulfil myself. We work through the parental material in order to be free of it and fulfil ourselves as inheritors of the previous generation's legacy.

The Work

- *List the primary dynamics about your relationship with your father. What did he or did he not fulfil of the father archetype for you? Strong? Insightful? Successful in the world? Aggressive, even domineering? Secure? Protective? Directed? Knowing the goal and doing what is necessary to achieve it? Or was he insecure, a wimp, withdrawn, cold, inadequate, ineffective, dominated by his wife or boss, unable to take stands on what he felt was real and right? Your work is cut out for you. The qualities that your father did not embody must still be developed in you. Are we assuming too much that the qualities he did embody are also developed in you? If not, look at why. Was he competitive with you and you early on gave up? Did he not encourage, especially if you are a woman, your strengths, power in the world, and decisiveness?*

- *Write a letter to your father which you do not necessarily send telling him all the things you would have liked him to have been but was not. Get free of the repression and disappointment. State your case and get on with it.*

- *What is the heritage from the father you need to come to terms with and live yourself? How can you obtain the blessing, the passing on of the birthright, the energy for your own full development and achievement in the world?*

- *See what dreams may bring as you work to accept your father rather than resist him. Look also at other people who have fathered you and helped make you strong and determined in this life. What next is there to do? Do it now, this coming year. It may be as practical as learning to drive a car or getting a job which uses more of your abilities than ever before, or studying long hours day and night to make something of yourself. Know that the ideal father would want you to achieve and help keep you at it. He would give you instruction about how things are not easy in this life, and ask you, why have so much less when you can have so much more? Follow the father-child dynamics and relationship as it develops in your dreams, and in your intimate relating with males, should that be occurring. We relate to others to relate to ourselves. Make sure you are milking your relationships creatively for everything they are worth. Learn how to be used well by others and to use others well yourself. The father goes for the value and never looks back!*

We heal by embodying what has been lost.

80 Healing the Mother Relationship

Image: *The woman washes her clothes at the well.*

'Simply touch with her heart.'

Do we ever heal the mother relationship? This is our bonding with life itself, the nurturing breast, the bloody womb that bore us and pushed us out to the music of agony, the wild hysterics of uncontrolled emotion, the gentle sensitivity, the trust that someone will always be there in life, later proven not to be true. And above all, the attachment to life itself even stronger than death. Chaucer writes in his early English poetry, 'With my staff I tap upon the ground three times and I say, "Ah, Mother Dear, let me in." ' So is that the return to the womb then, is that what sex is all about? The male appendage constantly seeking the nest which every woman has, however well or ill she uses it. The nest, the womb, the silken shaft, the passage of life, the tunnel to ecstasy, the withering womb of old age fast becoming tomb.

To a woman the mother is the only one who understands her, who is like her, yet older and either wiser or more debilitated than ever. The strong young woman learns what life has done to mother and will do to her if she is not conscious enough of life and its forces. The strong young woman is almost virginal and free, an adventurer, dancer to life's new beat, a bit of a wild one, seeking, always seeking. Gradually, though, she must yield to other forces, take the seed and give back to life a new generation. To care and be cared for, that is her hope, and how long does it last? So much bitterness can set in.

To heal the relationship with the mother, is it not to accept both the dark and the light side? Tell her what you have gone through and see if she responds. But also paint figures of the goddesses, the mother in all her aspects. Do not be caught up for too long in the personal mother whose own womanliness may have been too much fashioned in the image of man's desire. Find then the great mother and let the personal mother go. Have your talks but look for the healing and feminine elsewhere as well.

And when it comes to the end, the holy rite may well be sickness, a dark passion to match the light in many women. The bleeding womb, the body's own orifice, women have a thousand ways of needing healing. In your rite of sickness and support you will be closer, you will know mystery. Try to stay with the feelings, even the great anger should it present itself. That is you you see in her face.

The Work

- *Write a letter to your mother telling her how much you love her, whether you mean it or not. But really put yourself in the space of love. The extent to which you can express love to your mother is the measure of your capacity to love. So you need the testing and the practice. You do not have to send the letter, but you can express yourself in one.*

- *List some of the ways you feel you have wronged your mother. Put some heart into it. Give details and feelings. The picture which develops may well be the ways you have wronged the feminine mother part of yourself. So in recontacting the mother you are contacting the Source Mother within.*

- *Get time alone with your actual mother, even if you have to 'steal' her from your father. Your task is to seek that part of her which has a separate identity from that which she has built in relation to men. Also seek that part of her which is different from her mother role expressed towards you over the years. Now you will be finding the woman in her, and feeling connected in a way never possible before. You will be seeking an experience of affirmation of who you really are as a person.*

- *Do not write out the good and the bad about your mother, or all those things you need to forgive her for. This would be discriminating, using the categories of right and wrong. There is no right and wrong regarding the feminine. Only beingness, the free sharing of hurt and love, the freedom which comes with acceptance, the enthusiasm for life which comes from giving of oneself to that which matters, the sensitivity and simple wisdom that can be there in touch, cooking, and humour. If you must forgive, then forgive, let go of the past. But there is nothing to forgive her or anyone for unless you are stuck in categories of right and wrong, an activity more of the masculine. Simply touch with the heart. Don't analyse. Live!*

There is nothing to forgive where all is one.

195

81 Jealousy

Image: *The apple remains just out of reach.*

'No one can help the pup who does not fight for her share of the nipple'

'Why am I not getting my needs met?' asks the adult who was once upon a time a child within a family or in a group in the neighbourhood or at school.

The child knows that in order to survive she must enter into rivalry with others around her own age. She must compete. He must fight to survive. They must be aware whom the teacher favours and whom the parent likes. We know the favoured, do we not?

In this life no one will feed you unless your mouth is open and in the right place. That is your responsibility. If you are jealous, or wrapped in envy because someone else is getting what you are not getting, then you are in danger of losing in the struggle for life.

There are many who have tried and given up on relationships, or on making work that which expresses their true talent and creativity. Millions live intimately with someone whose very being does not allow their partners to be fulfiled in the relating. Many earn less than their neighbours and justify their near poverty with high ideals or economic theory, but where are they in the challenge to have the most fulfilling life possible? And the depressed ones who have almost given up living beyond the minimal level, what recourse have they? The Great Mother of Fulfilled Desire is not democratic, but she does give of what she has to those who demand for themselves.

If you are jealous of someone else, then they seem to have what you want but are not choosing to get for yourself. The problem is in you, not in their success. Are you committed to living passionately, expressing all of yourself in your struggle for life? No, you do not have to run over anyone to fulfil yourself, but you do need to be willing to be ahead, to be better than others in what you accomplish. Commit yourself to expressing your full potential in whatever you do and you need never be jealous again. The race goes to the winner, never the loser. There is no consolation prize in this reality.

The Work

- *Who told you not be be jealous or envious of another? Did it come from your parents or a religion? Why go against instinct and the need to do more than survive? A greater need is to fulfil oneself. List those attitudes which keep you from fulfilling yourself. Then list new attitudes as affirmations and intentions you will life by?*

- *Visualise yourself as one of a litter of too many pups for one mother dog to handle. Write up the fantasy and draw some conclusions about your behaviour and attitudes. What would you like to change? Do the visualisation a second time with really fulfilling behaviour for yourself.*

- *Is your natural disposition more to help others meet their needs, or to meet your own needs first? Look at this. It works better to focus initially on your needs and to act to meet them directly in a way that others involved can also get some of their needs met. In this way all or almost all benefit. There are enough victims in this world. You do not have to go around saving them all. Take care of yourself. Self-neglect creates jealousy and competitiveness. What is your pattern here? What will you do to transform it?*

Never hold back and you will lack nothing.

82 Fairness

Image: *An old man cracks eggs at the dinner table.*

'You did the right thing and you were rewarded.'

Most of us had a childhood in which we did not always get what we wanted, a childhood where doing the right thing was not always rewarded, where others acted out their own destructiveness and often seemed to obtain the goodies of life anyway. We might have been too honest, too kind, too considerate of others, and someone else took advantage of this and did us in to meet their own needs. We protested. We got upset. Even if we never said a thing in our own defence we secretly protested reality, we secretly thought that what was done to us was wrong.

As we were growing up we did not like the true stories we heard about people murdering each other and about the wars going on in the world. But our complaint was against our parents. Too often they insisted on getting their way with us. Too often they insisted on their views being the correct ones. We rebelled, either openly or inside ourselves. Life seemed unfair and we did not want to be here. We retreated into the realm of fantasy, or began acting out.

School seemed fair most of the time. If we studied and didn't make disturbances we would receive good grades. We did the right thing and we were rewarded. We were, unfortunately, being taught a false view of reality. There is no certain evidence that the just, the good, the ethical, receive greater benefits for their behaviour than the conniving, the underhanded, the politicians, the power-brokers, the business sharks.

Everyone seems to receive some of life's plenty whether they are particularly good or not.

So rather than a Judge of Fairness, there may well be in this life a swing and sway of opposites. It is possible that everyone receives good and bad in equal measure no matter how good they try to be. Is this fair? It is not fair but it is balanced.

To integrate childhood experience the second time around means to accept as a valid part of life the wrongs, the unfairness, which were done to us. To be abused, to lose a parent, to go through emotional or physical hell, shows the dark side balancing the times of health, being well parented, being emotionally sound. Your ego is biased towards the positive. Watch it! What you neglect will take you over.

If we insist that things should be different from how they are, we will create false reality pictures and do ourselves no good. No absolute fairness exists in life, simply reality and its consequences. No perfect universe exists other than the one we've got. If we build another one in our mind we will weaken our reality sense.

Some people become cynics and go for what they can get. Others appeal to saviours and parental figures to protect them from life. Still others act out of their inner victim to attract healing. The more conscious people accept good and evil as natural forces and seek to meld them into one whole. They redeem their childhoods by realising that whatever happened is consistent with the way the world works, and if they had a hard childhood they were not that prepared to deal with adversity. The more conscious expect opposites to occur and make realistic plans and processes for coping with both the light and the dark.

Wholeness means expressing all sides of oneself. We need to be consciously bad sometimes, to actualise that energy in life. Try not to be a victim of your own one-sidedness. Those who want only good bring evil upon themselves. This is the great law of opposites. In place of the fairness doctrine put the law of balancing the opposites by honouring and integrating both sides. If we substitute objectivity for fairness, life will go better for us.

The Work

- *What is your earliest memory or experience of the world not being fair, and what kind of reaction did that realisation produce in you?*

- *If you still expect people and situations to be fair, describe your own attitudes which might be producing this expectation.*

- *Are you using all the power available to you in your life? If not, what attitudes may be blocking your living to the fullest?*

Balancing opposites brings healing.

83 Forgiveness

Image: *Open hands cup the blood.*

'We are our own worst adversary, and that is where the issue
of forgiveness lies.'

I know that for most of us there is someone back there in the early
years who hurt us, and whom we do not want to forgive.

Although my parents gave me a hellish childhood, I can see purpose
and gentleness looking back at their actions. Perhaps their decision to
send me away wasn't so bad. Would it have been any better living
with them instead of living at boarding school? My wrath is more for
the military school teacher who suddenly yanked me out of my seat
and started beating me furiously about my head. But what is there to
forgive about such evil?

What is there to forgive for all the world's murderers and soldiers
who kill without decency? Many of us who have been victims would
rather fight back and kill our adversaries. But there are so many
adversaries in this life. If we could kill them all, who would be left?

We are our own worst adversary, and that is where the issue of
forgiveness lies. If I focus on the one I hate, the one in whom I see no
possibility for redemption, then I will never be able to forgive. If I
focus on myself, then the possibility is there to let go of the past, no
matter what is has been.

We do not forgive in the sense of absolving someone of a wrong
doing. Forgiveness is an act of sacrifice, an act of letting go of what
has already been taken from us. Those who cannot forgive are still
holding on to what should have been. What was, is reality. What
should have been never exists.

We let go of the past to be more fully in the present. Forgiveness is
redemption for myself, not another. Perhaps the energy will change
with the adversary also, but that is not within our control.

The process of forgiveness is to recall and experience the wounds
you received and who caused them. To feel what happened as a
necessity. We do not forgive through will power. We can only forgive
when we feel unable to forgive. There must be sacrifice. I must own
what I am letting go of. In most cases of resentment against parents it
is not necessary to encounter the actual parents. The parents of today
are not the parents of your childhood. The process of forgiveness is

an inner process of experiencing and letting go of the defensiveness surrounding your own wounds. We let go of seeing the world as one great adversary with others to blame for our own misfortune.

You are in fear of life until you can forgive. Remaining in old wounds at some point becomes an indulgence, becomes remaining identified with the Victim. To free yourself from the Adversary through forgiveness is to free yourself from identification with the Victim Archetype.

Perhaps light a candle, list the wrongs created by your adversaries, let yourself feel them without any longer being defensive about them, and then let go completely. Let go of the adversary and let go of being a victim. You may write a letter to your inner child or to your inner parents. And be in a sacred space where you cannot be disturbed and can experience healing, such as in nature or a place of meditation.

For myself, a few years ago in analysis I made my mother's head in clay and when the impulse came to me I destroyed it. What was wiped out in that piece of clay was her hold on me. Once I allowed expression of the worst I could go on to better. She became a fallible human being to me, not so much my mother any more. My new mother was alive inside me as I grew in feeling and expressed the nurturing and creative side in my life.

The Work

- *From what is described in the above text, create a procedure for yourself to forgive the adversaries of childhood. Perhaps you do not feel ready, or will do it more than once. Are we ever fully ready for the next step? Go through your process, either alone or with others, and write about what comes up.*

- *If you have not been able yet to go through the process of forgiveness, then list what is stopping you and look for healing dreams and experiences.*

- *'Forgive us our destructive acts as we forgive those who have been destructive towards us' comes from a well known religious text. Where does forgiveness come from according to this teaching? Is forgiveness, or redemption, a given as part of the universe or an act which comes from an arbitrary deity which must be importuned? What must we do? What must the source of forgiveness do? In order to be forgiven, or feel redeemed of past wounds, blocks, and even deliberate acts of evil or destructiveness, what must we do? The choice is to do what?*

- *Is there anything in life which a person cannot be forgiven for? On what basis? Is there always healing for every conflict or act of destructiveness?*

- *Now work on redeeming childhood by going through a forgiveness process, the rage, the hurt, the helplessness, the defensiveness which occurred as a result, the letting go of defensiveness and blocks, the choice to be freed of the past, the felt coming in of a healing power from other than ego, the shift in life perspective or world view, the commitment to living a new and transforming life.*

Those who forgive little will gain little.
Those who forgive much will have much.

84 Choice-Making

Image: *Lightning breaks out on a clear day.*

'We say Yes to one thing and No to all that would oppose it.'

I remember years ago visiting a friend of mine. Bedtime for their three year old came and they presented the child with choices. 'Do you want to go to bed now? Do you want a story read to you? Do you want some hot chocolate? Do you want your red pyjamas?' I hate to list the several more questions they asked their three year old. Finally he said, 'No, no, no, no, no!' to everything. The 'good' parents had overwhelmed their child with choices. They had tried to dump their own choice-making responsibility onto a child who was not at that level yet. They did not know the power and nature of choice-making. Nor did they realise that choosing against is not the same as choosing for something.

Choice-making appears to be one of the most neglected areas of life. Where are the courses and books on the subject? Every day of our lives we make choices, yet how many of us have the skills for this activity?

One key to effectiveness is the ability to make choices. A choice is putting energy in one direction and not another. We say 'Yes' to one thing and 'No' to all that would oppose it.

Many of us are more attracted to saying 'Yes' than 'No', and then after a while all the Yeses we have said overwhelm us. Stress comes from having said 'Yes' without saying 'No'. Fewer people say 'No' more often than 'Yes' in life. Saying 'No' can be creative if in saying 'No' we are opening ourselves to the possibility of saying 'Yes'. Better to say 'No' than an automatic 'Yes' which we do not carry out.

But there are those, very guarded perhaps, who mostly say 'No' or say nothing. The No-sayers may need to be more open to life's possibilities and risk more. If caught in a bind and ambivalence, start choosing, saying 'Yes' to things over and over again. Such a practice will break the pattern and give you plenty of consequences to deal with.

Perhaps you feel that the Universe is always saying 'No' to you and therefore you must protect yourself by also saying 'No' to the Universe? Who will break this cycle first? You or the Universe? You have the power of choice. You break the pattern first!

When we are about seventeen many of us begin making our own choices as to how to live our lives. We are still dependent, yet want to be independent. We know that within a year or two we will be more or less out on our own in life. We no longer take the parents' opinions as the right opinions about life. We rebel, or go against. We want to make our own choices. This is the birth of the creative ego in the seventeen year old, the birth of a distinct personality willing to go against the parents to find him or herself. Choice in this case is the demarcation line between self-identity and family expectations.

Many of us who did not develop creative ego in the late teens, as adults learn to have our own perceptions and opinions, and to make our own choices. We learn to take the consequences regardless of what others say. No one can make your choices for you. You sink or swim yourself.

The Work

- *When did you start making choices for yourself? Describe the dynamics and what you learned about life from the experience. Perhaps the first ones were more in the No category? Perhaps there were some great Yes choices, say regarding love relationships? What were the consequences and how did you deal or not deal with them? Did you feel you got burned, that you were not ready for choice? How has your high school experience coloured your attitudes towards choices and their consequences?*

- *What are some of the major choices you are needing to make at the present time? What is your choice-making process? Your underlying attitudes? The alternatives in the situation? What you like and dislike? The greatest potential and value in the situation? The sense of appropriate timing? The larger perspective? The specific immediate choices needing to be made? Your commitment to dealing with the consequences?*

- *Write out a procedure for choice-making from beginning to end.*

What we choose is what we become.

85 Graduating from School

Image: *The vase of old flowers is thrown into the air.*

'To graduate is to close the door to the past and take only the essence with you.'

Graduation at last! We are going out into the world. The tune, 'Pomp and Circumstance' runs through my ears. I experience transcendence and joyful sadness. As a march, it moves me forward in life. As a feeling experience, it allows me to look backwards for the last time.

Until now we have been part of a family and peer group. At graduation we go out into the world as an individual to find our own friends and way of life. Some of us will stay close to home and the familiar habits we have known. Others will go even thousands of miles away into different lifestyles. This is the parting of the ways. To celebrate is to honour the transition. We are being required by the prod of time to move on.

Turn and look forward now. The future we must anticipate. The future is always where life lies.

Will I let go of the past? Will I embrace the transition despite fears? Do I have a sense of the heroic? Have I taken stock of myself and my ability to interact in the world?

Graduation. It happens every so often in life. A major job or relationship ends. Have I learned the lesson, or am I upset because of all the missed opportunities? To graduate is to close the door to the past and take only the essence with us. Its lesson is how to let go so that we can open ourselves to the future.

How we graduate affects all the other transitions in our lives. If we never leave childhood we will have a hard time accepting the next turning points on the way. Moving to another place or city, making a marriage and a family, welcoming the birth of a child without too much regret or fear, choosing meaningful work, committing to the spiritual journey, dealing with children leaving home, making a major vocation change, accepting severe illness, experiencing the peak of one's life and career, dealing with dying and death, these are all major transitions affected by how we did or did not leave childhood. Leaving childhood is the first great transition. If we did not go through a sufficient initiation process into life, in all the subsequent transitions we will be reliving the original attempt at graduating into life, including the fears and resistances we hardly dealt with the first time around. Better to finally graduate than to hang on forever fearful of the next stages in life.

Let us celebrate all the stages in life!

The Work

- *Write up your graduation experience as it was for you. Then write it as you would have liked it to have been.*

- *These are the essentials of the graduation experience:*
    - *Anticipating the new, the next stage in life*
    - *Wanting to regress, to stay on at the present stage or even go backwards to an earlier time in your life*
    - *Honouring what has been by bringing it to essence*
    - *Honouring through recall who you were, where you started, and how far you have come*
    - *Feeling afraid of the future, the dangers, the new*
    - *Sensing the grand adventure of moving into new life*
    - *Practising self-definition*
    - *Listing one's skills, personality characteristics and accomplishments so far in life*
    - *Formalising the transition with self-reflection, ceremony and celebration with friends and significant others*
    - *Choosing new life*
    - *Dealing with the common side of life which will come afterwards to ground you again in the everyday tasks of existence.*

- *If you have been to any class reunions, what feelings and issues came up for you? How have you grown?*

- *What are your attitudes toward transition and renewal? Which ones need changing? What are some new affirmations or attitudes which you would like to practise on this theme?*

- *Much additional suffering is caused by resistance to change. How does this dynamic affect your life?*

- *What do you need to graduate from at the present time?*

For the living there is no death, only transition.

86 Compromise With Reality

Image: *The black king snake suns himself on a large rock.*

'This good earth is the arena of the real.'

Let's face it. Many of us do not at times want to be here. Reality seems a difficult if not horrible place to exist. The stresses and strains get us down. We have major gifts, great thoughts, but we don't quite seem to make it in this world. We wish it were simpler. Perhaps if we were more hardy, more intelligent, not who we are, things would go better? Maybe if we hadn't had the difficult childhood we had, the parents we had, it would go better?

But we are in the present moment. We live with this reality, whatever the handicaps. One person is sick much of the time, allergic to this and to that. Another has been affected with amenorrhea, the inability to menstruate, and feels handicapped as a woman. Someone else is born into a wealthy family and feels neglected enough to consider suicide. A child who dreamed over and over again of being on crutches following Jesus later developed polio, was confined to a wheelchair, and became a nun. Some hide out in their rooms as children. Others escape the house of tension whenever they can. Still others are beaten, sexually molested, not understood. Reality hurts, and sometimes hurts badly.

Do we want to be here? Is the adult life, where we hope to have more choice, any more free and fulfilling than a rough childhood?

The way out is the way through. This life of ours is the arena of the possible, the one place to be. Be here now. If you can give up your idealism, your longing, your values which are too high, your compulsive fears, then you have a chance to live a fulfilling life. But you must choose to be here. Make as strong a choice as you can to create your choices within the arena of the possible. The preliminary requirement for making this great choice is to have acknowledged and worked through the central aspects of your childhood.

Yes, make your compromise with reality. You will know those who have made a similar commitment to yours by their human quality. They can look you in the eye. They have a ready response to every moment, every issue. They take joy and suffering alike in equal value. They do not hide behind any trappings, religious, family, work, neurosis, friendship or the like. They exist as people in their own right and treat you as an individual capable of a similar consciousness. When you are around such people your own awareness expands and good choices come out of nowhere. You feel the centre within the other person and seem to respond naturally from your own centre within. There is no complaining. There are only choices and their consequences.

This good earth is the arena of the real. Deal with it. Welcome to reality! Welcome to life!

The Work

- *Why not continue to resist the real? List the ways you can still resist your life. How can you improve on them, become even more defensive and unreal. Devise a grand plan.*

- *Describe the defence system you built up in childhood for resisting the way things were. Did you fantasise a different world? Write down your imaginary world. Behind the symbols are the seeds of your future life, the potentials for healing a sick childhood.*

- *Are you a controller or a fantasiser? Are you selecting certain segments of your life and repressing others you fear? Go where the fear is. There you will find the ego dangerously close to non-acceptance of reality. Change your attitude at the fear place. Begin the new approach with 'I accept things just as they are and I will . . . .'*

- *When you are almost ready, devise a simple ceremony or meditation which indicates your choice to enter fully into this world as it truly is. This is your compromise with reality, this is your grand choice to be as real as you can. Perhaps your choice might include the following elements.*
    - *I will live as fully as I can in the present moments as they come.*
    - *I will attempt not to space out into the past or the future as I make my daily choices.*
    - *I choose to be here. This is the arena of my life to be lived now. I am choosing to be alive to each moment as it comes. I will find my fulfilment in the potentials which come my way, not in fantasies or other forms of unconsciousness.*
    - *I will work not to repress unpleasant experiences, but to process them with an ongoing commitment to*

wholeness. I want to be fully alive, and to participate passionately in the world.

- *I will gradually cease those destructive practices which make me go unconscious as an avoidance of reality. Any substance which alters my perception of reality as it is and weakens my ability to choose at an everyday level is likely to be destructive to my choice-making.*
- *I will live passionately including life's opposites. I will not leave out the dark side. I am alive now, and that is what counts.*

Reality heals us as it wounds us!

87 The Letter

Dear people in my childhood,

My mother, Gene Derwood, my father, Oscar Williams, Richard and Diana, brother and sister, friends of mine, Miss Day, my best teacher, and all the other supportive teachers and friends.

I needed you, and perhaps you needed me. Parents chose not to raise me and so I respond to all of you.

This is a letter of goodbye to the good and the bad. I have returned to childhood to experience and process what was there. Now I let it go. I give up the traumas and resentments. I laugh at them. They did not do me in and I am now very much alive. True, I still have bouts of sickness, nausea just as in childhood. I am having a severe bout right now. I am amazed at how much suffering I can take. And I also look forward to healthier times. I don't ever expect to be completely cured of childhood. That would be perfection. I am willing to live the suffering which comes my way.

And what have I gained from childhood which I take with me? My ruggedness, my ability to persist despite all odds. A devotion to healing in God, in myself and in others. God, or Source, seems to have much darkness and imperfection. How else can I explain the bad stuff which happened to me. Why should I exclude anything;

Time once again to move on. I have been there and returned, hopefully with more compassion and consciousness this time round. And I thank others who have travelled with me. We have journeyed into and out of childhood together.

My love, my parents, my children, my friends and enemies, are alive in me. I shall sign this letter with all of the names of my heritage. Good-bye!

Strephon Derwood Kaplan-Williams

88 Graduating from Childhood

Image: *Receiving a black cloth and a golden staff.*

'We are here. There is no where else we can possibly be.'

What follows must be taken with self-acceptance on all our parts. Do we, can we, in fact graduate from childhood? How we have survived childhood deeply affects the rest of our lives, no matter how much we put ourselves through self-transformation. Yet there are certain fundamentals which can indicate what the real graduation from childhood is like.

The Fundamentals

• A person who has graduated from childhood seldom complains about anything. To complain is to be critical and non-accepting of something without doing anything about it. At the root this complaining is a statement that the complainer's childhood should have been different from how it was. Not having accepted childhood exactly as it was means that we still have grounds for complaint. We don't like something and wish it were different. We want things to be other than they are. Furthermore, the true complainer never makes much effort to change the conditions which cause the complaint.

In childhood we were faced with things which caused us pain and we were helpless to do anything about most of them. The adults had the power. The only way we could resist was by crying, pouting, throwing a tantrum. If we didn't develop a strong sense of choice as we grew up, we continued to feel powerless in the face of adversity. We continued to complain. In adult life when opposed we complain. We have awful husbands, governments, world conditions, head-aches, and so on. The point is not to complain about any of these conditions but to do something about them. If you feel something is wrong, change it! If you can't change it, change yourself! And what if you cannot change what you consider an oppressive situation or person? Then accept reality as it is or get out. Why be involved in any situation which you do not have the power to influence or change?

• The mature adult makes his or her compromise with reality. How many of us have accepted being here on earth? Are we still resisting anything in life? It's difficult not to wish for things we don't have. As children we always wished for something better than we got. Now we have entered adult life and we are still wishing for things to be different. We construct in our minds an ideal reality with which to evaluate and flee from the real world. If you are resisting anything in this life you have not yet made your compromise with reality. You still want a better lover than you've got, more money than you have, a different place to live, to be a different sex. You name it, somebody has wished for it.

To make our compromise with reality is to work within its confines. We accept what is and create with it. We live in the arena of the possible. We live now, not later. Whatever life we have, we have now. We are here. There is nowhere else we can possibly be.

• For the mature adult the parents no longer exist as parents. They are people now. The children as adults owe them nothing and are owed nothing. Your parents are the old life. You are moving into the new. Let them be. Let them go. Move on.

Parents have no special rights over their grown children. People will take the most outrageous things from parents which they would never take from their closest friends. The adult child is still afraid of offending the parent because in childhood the parents played the power game and broke their children, instilling fear in them because of their use of power. If you are afraid of offending your parents in any way, shape or form you have not yet become an adult.

• We choose not to form dependency relationships as places to hide in adult life. In actuality we all form dependency relationships, but these in our modern era often split up with much suffering on both sides.

What happens of course is that the umbilical cord is severed once again in a relationship dissolution. The cord will be severed if it is a dependency relationship. It may be severed anyway. Through sex we establish the umbilical cord to The Mother, our partner of either sex, and when the relationship breaks we cry out, re-experiencing the agony of original loss. In addition to being an instinctive response, wanting sex is wanting re-attachment to The Mother for renewal or regression from adult life. Successfully solving the dependency syndrome means that we are living our own lives in as many ways as we can, including financially, sexually, in friendship, and in personal growth. No longer will the partners play amateur therapists to each

212

other, although they will support each other's own needs, and thereby be more able to support their partner in meeting his or her needs.

• We are committed to working through dependency issues whenever they come up. While we may not be in a dependency relationship, we will have surges of dependency arising from the past or from present stress. We must in these cases take our courage in our hands and support our own growth instead of expecting our partners to meet our needs.

• We do not resist life transitions but celebrate them meaningfully. Because we have made a transition out of childhood in working through our material, we are able to meet and take hold of all the other transitions in life.

The people who have the hardest time dying have never left childhood. They want to stay alive because they have never lived. They then have to work through all the dependency issues in dying that they should have worked through years earlier. They experience the archetypal wounded child in their own sickness once again, and finally, they may have numinous experiences of the wondrous child as they die. It seems paradoxical that the dying experience should be a final return to childhood experience, but if you have not grown up of course you must go back to the beginning in order to face your ending.

• We commit to living from the Divine Child archetype, the archetype of the Self. We live a new essence daily. We are spontaneous beings, flexible and resilient to the end of our days. We have vitality and consciousness. A manifestation of spiritual power shows in much of what we do. We have made ourselves a vehicle for a larger process than ego, a larger process than even our parents hoped or expected for us. We do not live out our parents' expectations. We do not live out our own expectations. We live the potentials of the central archetype, parented now by the sources of the universe. We are reborn daily into life. We choose to protect and nurture that new birth through daily action.

• If we have already graduated from childhood we welcome death when it comes as an ultimate experience of transition. We do not fear to die because we have achieved a major adult task, which is to leave childhood dependency behind and finally live from the Divine Child, the central archetype of the Self. Death then becomes an experience of divinity in which we feel ourselves as the child of God, one who has

213

been given the supreme gift of life, realised it, and now exits this world.

The Work

- *Write a letter of commitment to yourself covering in your own words each of the above points. Once finished, you might even send it in the mail to yourself. And certainly read it in a Transforming Childhood group if you are in one.*

- *Write a chronology of your life right through childhood to the age of twenty-one. Name each year and list or write up one or two of the most important events and their significance. This becomes in part your Myth of Childhood, your inner as well as outer journey.*

We move on by realising the significance of the events we have been through.

214

89 Saying Goodbye

Image: *A pitcher filled with clear water and two glasses.*

'But I choose not to remain there.'

This is our ceremony. The time has come, as time moves on, to leave that first early period of childhood. I have returned there in many ways and been moved by many things. But I choose not to remain there. The future again calls me onward to life. I am to say good-bye. I am to let go of that period of my life as I acknowledge once again who I was and will never again be. Yet in leaving I may take the essence with me, the core of my destiny to live now.

I say goodbye to all that was.

I say goodbye to the small child.

I say goodbye to the parents who loved me and found me difficult.

I say goodbye to the wounds and the joys back then.

I say goodbye to all I did and did not get.

I say goodbye to my little child self.

I see you now. I hug and embrace you. I let go of all that was then because my heart is changing.

I see you, yet I let you go, I must move on.

The Work

- *The above ceremonial refrain can be used as an honouring and a letting go process in order to help bring further resolution to that period of our lives. In our 'saying goodbye' ceremony we toast the past, say the child's name, and read the refrain. So now please read over the refrain and use it as a suggestion for writing your own refrain to say at the ceremony. Take it as far as you can, knowing that there is still, and maybe always will be, more early childhood material to work through. Perhaps see the small child you as you write or say the refrain.*

- *Allow your feelings and images to be present to you. What was once overwhelming can now be cleansing. Feel the support. Feel the family and strength of the adult years. The new sustenance and community are all those who journey with you, who are committed at various levels to developing the inner way and achieving consciousness and wholeness.*

In ending, experience beginning!

Death-Rebirth

For every season there is a choice.
A time to die and a time to live.
A time for decrease and a time for increase.
For every beginning there is an ending.
A time for regression and a time for growth.
A time for saying goodbye and a time for saying hello.

For anything new the old must go.
A grave to be dug and new seed planted.
A sacrifice made as well as fulfilment created.

The days of our years are numbered by eternity.
What was will never again be.
The songs which have been sung are only an echo.

We are as grains of sand in the infinitude of oceans.
Our consciousness illuminates life for only an instant.
We are nothing in a transcendent now.

And what we have we have not.
What we are we will not be.
What we can become is already
A burden on our shoulders.

Where is my life going? asks the seeker.
To what end are all my choices?
And for what purpose have I been born or unborn?

Yet still will I say my refuge is in what is.
My salvation is in what I do with what life brings me.
My longing is within the sacred.

When I am no more the rains will still fall.
The seasons will swirl into eternity.
And the voice of my lips will be somebody's song.

For I am not alone in my common humanity.
I am not alone in the journey towards wholeness.
I am at peace where the centre guides me.
And I shall live in all my dying.

Appendix I
Quick Reference
Guide

Use this guide to look up quickly a particular emotion, feeling, or issue you are dealing with right now in your life. This may help you gain perspective.

1. Abuse – The doing to anyone, but especially a child, of harm psychologically or physically. The issue is using superior force to get your way. Extreme abuse is violent or sexual and creates fear and withdrawal in the child so that he or she becomes afraid of interacting with adults. But many parents are abusive to their children when they insist on winning the power game by making their children do things rather than giving them choices and alternatives for action. Abused children often become abusive adults. To heal this condition work in therapy to get to the anger and hurt resulting from your own childhood. Express these deep emotions and feelings in new creative ways and thus become free of their compulsive quality. You can express frustration without having to take it out on somebody.

2. Anger – *Anger is the emotion of repressed feeling.* It takes energy to repress energy. The defensive personality represses feelings and emotions which eventually explode when our buttons are pushed. The first stage of anger is repression. We do not even know we hurt or are angry. The second stage is expression. We know we are angry because it suddenly comes up and we express it. But we are not yet in touch with the hurt and issues behind the anger. The third stage is anger transformation. We know we are angry, express it immediately in a creative way, get to the feelings and issues behind the anger, and resolve the issue and situation right away when appropriate. We become less angry and more expressive of feelings, positive and negative.

3. Anxiety – *Anxiety is fear without an object.* To cure anxiety list all the specific things you might be afraid of and devise ways of dealing with them. Anxiety is always about the future based on the past. We did not deal well with something and now we are afraid again of its happening. We fear what might happen, not what is actually happening if we are fully present. Being fully in the moment means you are aware and acting in the moment. No time for anxiety since you are active. To cure anxiety ACT and never look back.

4. Attitudes – *Attitudes are unconscious rules for living life.* They are the contexts within which we make our choices. In childhood the adults repeated to us over and over again rules, or attitudes, for how to live life. These attitudes may be realistic or actually lead to not being effective in life. Our task with childhood material is to root out the unconscious attitudes our parents and society gave us, take a good look at them, and decide whether we want to live from those attitudes or not. What may have been true for previous generations may no longer be fulfilling for the present generation. *You get free of childhood by deciding for yourself which attitudes and principles you will live by.* Also, the traumas of childhood which were not dealt with other than defensively create attitudes, such as the world is a dangerous place to live, only partly true of course.

5. Beginnings – Starting something new will always spark off a similar childhood dynamic. How we wake up each morning is the way we were born into life. If you feel a special anxiety over starting something new, look to your childhood experiences and work them through again. In every present act we repeat the childhood act. Get free, see the part the past plays in the present and then choose what is best in the present based on the reality of what is happening now, not what happened 'way back when'.

6. Body – Our physical being, the image of which has usually been distorted in our childhood experiences. Were we made to feel that any bodily function was somehow bad and to be kept hidden? The new way is to accept and talk freely about any bodily function including elimination, illness and sex. There is no difference. It is all body. It is all us. The problem of love is also the problem of the love of the body. If you do not love your body as it is, you do not love. You cannot love another without loving yourself as well. For love of another would be only a projection of the need to love and honour yourself. We love our bodies when we take care of them, when we do not overwork them, forget our awareness of them, when we give the body exercise and do not put bad things into it from superfluous medications to dangerous substances. We love our bodies by staying in them and feeling them fully. To love oneself in the body is to be able to love another in the body. The body thrives on love, the acceptance of the body as it is in all its functions and parts. Through working on our bodies for healing we also work out our childhoods.

7. Child – The child is the natural part of us with terrific potential for growth and new life. The childhood problem is that most of us had to give up being the full child and became adults in attitude and behaviour too soon. So adults learning to play and be creative again will at first feel awkward because they have to first regress to that early age, six perhaps, when they closed off to being a fully expressive child. As adults allow the

220

child out whenever you can. This will be your source for renewal and joy in life. If not dealt with consciously the child will come out in compulsions and moodiness, not exactly the best way to lead a fulfilling life.

8. Choice – *Choice is directing energy in one direction and not another.* As children the adults often tried to make our choices for us. In this they greatly erred. For the child needs to develop as much choice-making as possible in order to enter adult life. Present alternatives to the child, not absolutes, unless of course it is for safety. We were probably never taught the fundamental skill of making choices and dealing with consequences. Time now as adults to learn the process and live it.

9. Commitment – *Commitment is sustained choice in a given direction over a definite amount of time.* There is a kind of knowledge which can only be gained through maintaining a commitment. For to go through the regressive pull, that which would divert us from our chosen paths, we must maintain a sustained choice no matter what comes up to divert us.

10. Communication – Communication, the sharing of ourselves with another, is one thing we found difficult in childhood. for many of us learned that if we shared our real selves, even with our parents, they would betray us, causing us to retreat. So the message from childhood is, be careful what you share. You may get hurt if you are too open. Yet in adult relationships holding back information or parts of ourselves leads to difficulties in maintaining the relationship. *Better to communicate and process rather than hold back and repress.*

11. Conflict – *Conflict is a situation of opposing forces.* Conflict is positive in the sense that it can lead to further differentiation among all parties involved. Normally we seek unity in life, in ourselves and with others. But too much or too prolonged a unity means merger and loss of personal identity. Thus struggle and conflict enter the picture to separate out the various parts of a unity. The old way was to try to resolve differences through one party wiping out the other party, as in most sports and in all wars. *The new way is to balance opposing forces so that they can differentiate without one having to destroy the other. This is struggle within unity.* In terms of childhood most parents tried to win out over their children in forcing them to do things. Or one parent dominated another. As in childhood so in adult life. We do not know how to deal creatively with conflict because our parents never did. Learn now and become free of the past.

12. Creativity – The source of creativity is the Inner Child, that part of us which is spontaneous and radically open to the new in life, unbound by the old. Creativity is finding new solutions to old problems, and requires openness to any possibility and the willingness to change one's own point of view. First we accept the situation as it is, then we create with the energy,

221

going for new ways of resolution and manifesting potential.

13. Death – *The essence of the death experience is the necessity to let go of life.* Whatever we try to hold on to will be taken from us anyway, one way or another. So why not practise letting go? If however we have felt really deprived in childhood we will have learned to compulsively grasp on to things in order to feel safe and satisfy ourselves. We hold on to the old, afraid of the new. Death then challenges us as to the ultimate letting go, the letting go of our bodies and life itself. *Life is the goal of life and dying the process.* The natural child accepts death, that something has ended, been destroyed, acknowledges it, and then moves on to new life. We can do the same by practising daily letting go of life and letting go to life. Whatever we are attached to shackles us from doing other things which are also life giving. Our attachments are often residual needs from childhood. These needs must surface and be dealt with in order to have more freedom and to be less bound by our compulsions and deep seated desires. *Free the child and you free the adult.*

14. Defensiveness – Each of us grew up in childhood encased in a defence system with the wound of childhood carefully hidden at the centre. We learned to exist by defending ourselves, not by opening up to life. But all castles become prisons. *The walls which keep strangers out keep us in*, thus becoming strangers to ourselves through lack of self expression. To be defensive is to try and maintain that one is right and entitled to having needs met no matter what. We do not open, but resist reality as it is. We have not yet accepted our childhoods so we cannot accept adult life and reality itself. We act defensively, ready always for some adversity to come in at us. We lose sight of the new potential which may be there for us if we can just let go and go with.

15. Depression – *Depression means lack of energy due to repression.* Growing up in a difficult childhood means that we are defensive and depressed. We are using vital energy to hold down vital energy in ourselves. This means we have much less life energy available for life tasks. We are depressed and feel a lack of enthusiasm about the world and existence itself. To work it through we must get to the anger, the protest about childhood, express it, get to the wound and hurt of childhood surfacing in similar situations in adult life, and work all this through. Also, get moving, keep doing everyday things as well as working in movement and art. It is important to at least take what energy you do have and make creative ego choices with it. Just because you are depressed, do not assume that your attitude is right.

16. Ego – To the child the moment of realising personal identity is a major experience. At the beginning we seem to be merged with our family and surroundings. At first we say we, and then later we say I. The I is the differentiation of ego out of the primordial family archetype, the original

222

wholeness. We often begin by saying No, by resisting others' input to develop a sense of our own being and attitude towards things. We create images of ourselves, much as children put on make-believe costumes and play characters from life. We take on a set of attitudes, little rules for living life. We have sensory experiences from our body. And we begin the exercise in self-definition which is life long. We say what we like to eat and what we don't. We say who we are. We separate out from the parents gradually if natural processes of development are allowed to unfold. We gain more and more control over aspects of ourselves and life. We learn to create and to co-operate. But the adult crisis comes later for some or many of us because we did not keep developing an independent and strong ego. We regressed into roles in business and family life to make things easier. We found adult life even more difficult than childhood. So now more than ever we need to give up a weak, egocentric ego for a strong, creative ego in the service of the fuller Self, the centre of all life and its meaning.

17. Elated – The feeling of a burst of new energy, sometimes due to inflation with a new potential. This can show us the way to go. We feel a rise in energy, so why not do it? Fair enough. But feeling strong energy needs grounding in the everyday. How will I both express and create with my sense of new found energy?

18. Enemies – *We need our enemies, those who oppose us, for they are often there to humble us*. Adversaries in childhood often sought to overwhelm us, so we fear them. Who wants to be knocked out of existence in some way? Yet every enemy has something to teach us. For the adversarial energy comes in with a different viewpoint and use of power from our own. The greater flexibility is to blend with your adversary, using his or her energy to good effect. *The secret is to take on yourself what you most dislike in someone else*. If we are upset by opposition that must mean we have a onesided position which is not including its opposite. So along comes someone else to highlight and humble us. *The enemy is within*. It is called our shadow. The more we relate to our shadow as us the less we will be dominated by it and therefore needlessly create enemies. Be real rather than good, realistic rather than idealistic, integrative rather than onesided.

19. Family Archetype – The Family Archetype is a projected wholeness of the actual family, causing people to play roles in order to fulfil it. Thus we get all sorts of strivings, say for family unity, who plays mother and who father, the good child and the bad child, even the dog and the cat are included to represent the instincts and feeling function. But trying to live out roles does not allow individual wholeness, and so individuals in the family rebel against the structure, upsetting the rest of the members who are trying to preserve family wholeness by living out their allotted roles and attitudes. Any group formed will recreate the Family Archetype, and those involved will start acting out their original childhood roles again, seeking or being

223

parents, becoming the child, developing dependencies, conforming, rebelling, and the works. Supposedly sane, modern adults degenerate into the family of origin when the process gets heavy in a group. To integrate, keep withdrawing the wholeness projection from the family, both your original family and the new 'families' you create. Refuse to live out roles for yourself and others. Turn roles into functions which you have choice about.

20. Fantasy – Fantasy is the images of the mind. In childhood many of us went into fantasy as a special retreat from a harsh or rejecting reality. We found the realm of images and feelings much more alive and real than the drab oppressive exteriors of our actual childhood. This is a creative place to be for the child, and shows how strong the life urge is. However, in adult life we need to leave the fantasy world and bring its potential into outer reality. *What we dream about we can actualise if we will but open ourselves and make the effort.* Fantasy leads the way, showing us possibilities and what the psyche wants. But it also imprisons us if we refuse to leave the security of images and enter the concreteness of matter. One bird in the hand is worth a hundred in a dream bush. It may not be as pretty, but it is more real.

21. Father – Whether we had a real father or not, just as there is the biological father there is the psychological or inner one. *The adult task is to learn more and more to parent ourselves.* We turn image into function. See what of the masculine your actual father lived and did not live. We need role models. Did other significant males carry some of the father for you as a child? Are you in adult relationships seeking aspects of the father not realised in childhood? This would be natural. For we spend our lives seeking and relating to parental substitutes so that we may begin to realise these energies inside ourselves. That is the task, to heal the broken archetype, the partially realised parent inside, by exploration and living fully all of the parental functions ourselves. Or at least find good substitutes if you are not quite ready yourself to live a certain quality fully.

22. Fears – *Fear is the perception of possible loss.* We have not lost anything yet, from life to a bought object or keys. But we are afraid of losing something and so often inhibit ourselves from risking living a new life. The unconscious reaction to fear is to contract. Contraction freezes us and severely limits our ability to interact with what is seeking to harm or destroy us or our things. Better to tremble and shake in the face of adversity, for at least that releases energy which may be the preparation for activity and movement. Still better would be centred coping with what is difficult in the moment, doing this without fear but with a lively consciousness. *Fear is being afraid of that which does not yet exist.* If we are fully in each moment we will not be afraid and will act without fear. Whatever happens will be a success because we have fully given ourselves to the moment that is. A good preparation for being this centred is to practise letting go of anything to which we become attached. Attachment is what limits us. If we are identified with something or someone, and therefore afraid of experiencing a loss, we will limit ourselves. You must act as if the deep relationship you have, the object you have bought or created, the life you live, will be gone tomorrow, if not sooner. For in fact what happens tomorrow is going to be new and not a repetition of today. Let even the good stuff go, as you live vitally and without fear. *Voluntary sacrifice is the only true insurance there is.*

23. Feelings – In childhood most of us repressed our feelings because the parents and other authorities were trying to suppress them for us. They liked us when we were positive, when we loved Mummy and Daddy. But they disapproved when we hated them, when we were upset and misbehaving in public. So the message that came across was that you are only allowed to have good feelings, missing the point that feelings are feelings, whether good or bad. Just as there are positive and negative electrical charges so there must be feelings which are either positive or negative. This means it is natural to feel sad, angry, hurt, depressed, anguished, as well as ecstatic, happy, enthusiastic and warm. To find your feeling function again, which is the primary function needed for intimate relating, we need to go back to the natural child before he or she was cut off in childhood. But to get to the natural child we need to experience again the wounded child. Now in adult life we must learn to unite them again. We do this by expressing both positive and negative feelings as they come up. We give up trying to control our feelings by intellectualising and such compulsions as smoking. At last we are able to feel again, our personal connection in the moment to life.

24. Friendships – Friendships form in childhood for mutual support, though many times the energy seems to go more one way. One child becomes the follower and the other the leader. We may pick as a friend someone who has developed a characteristic we have not yet developed, like dating the opposite sex. Or we may use someone, or be used by someone, to talk about our lives. This is natural therapy. See whether you are a receiver-listener or a giver-entertainer in the relationship. Try to reverse roles. You may lose that friendship, but then seek another which is more balanced. For what we are going for is companionship, the relationship of sharing a common purpose. We are in relationship to learn and to teach. Never stay in a relationship when it no longer has potential to teach you about life. Simply supporting each other is not enough since it replicates the dependency syndrome from childhood. Seek friends who offer and want to receive new life and you will be more on the path.

25. Goals – Many of us had the goal of growing up and leaving childhood as fast as we could. We learned in school and home to concentrate on something outside ourselves, the goal, as the focus for achievement. Very early in life we were thrown off the track by being taught to focus outside ourselves instead of developing inner awareness and direction in life. The key, besides raw talent, to those who become major contributors to culture is that usually from very early on, they were already inner directed. They knew who they were and what they were doing. They were not focused on the future but on a strong destiny happening through them now, not later. So fashion your goals to be immediate, tangible, and related to your inner life as well. With every outer achievement make sure you have an inner one as well.

27. God – God, in terms of childhood, is the repository for all the parental energy we failed to receive from our actual parents. Very few children have parents who are themselves already fulfilled and therefore capable of encouraging fulfilment in their children. So a legacy grows of all the qualities we failed to find in our parents. God will save us from sin, wrath, sex, greed, violence, sickness, and the like. God will give us love, is all powerful and all knowing, and will heal us if we are worthy. What is this stating but that in the actual family there was anger, alcoholism, greed, neglect, weakness, lack of love, cunning, disrespect, and so on. Even if your family went to church or temple, you knew as a child that the dark side was being hidden or not expressed in a healthy way in the family. So now in adult life people are still faced with a harsh reality and still seek that ideal reality and parent, God, the kingdom of the elect, and finally paradise when this weary, hard life is ended. The corrective is to find God, or Source, or Healing, or Whatever, now in your immediate situation and in you. Leave too much dependency and enter into co-creation in which you aid the process as well as being aided by it.

27. Guilt – *The core of the guilt experience is when we have failed our own potential, not another.* You cannot fail others, even if you do not do what they want, even if you cannot do what you have promised. To have failed oneself is what gnaws at us because it creates the unlived life. The kiss lost, the opportunity not taken, these can never be lived again. And so we experience existential guilt at having failed the moment and ourselves. Others will try to make us feel guilty for having failed them or hurt them in some way. We are all trained from birth to say we are sorry. Sorry for what? We have not done anything wrong because we have failed another. Little children do not apologise. They are made to apologise by their parents. So they grow up feeling vaguely afraid because someone else is upset by their natural behaviour when they themselves have simply accepted their own imperfections as inherent to life. So in failing others, and being made to feel we are bad people because of it, we learn to be afraid of risking. Seeing ourselves as already bad, the feeling of guilt, we do not risk a new life and so genuinely fail ourselves where we could have actualised anew. To cure the problem, always affirm yourself and your point of view no matter what the others are saying about you. Let them have their reactions but not their judgements about you. Affirm yourself as you accept imperfection, then move on to the next choice, risking whatever is necessary to make it.

28. Happiness – Were you happy as a child? Most people might say yes, until they actually got into their childhood material. In order to feel happy we repress the unpleasant aspects of life. So the child hides suffering from itself because the parents do not accept the child's suffering. Most people learn to create a state of happiness by repressing hurt and suffering. This work is done in childhood by creating happy fantasies, and then as we grow up, by sex, drugs, medicine, eating, spacing out, over-talking or work. This experience of happiness is not based on health, and therefore contributes to illness by masking pain so effectively that the person can avoid dealing with the causes of the mental pain. Parents most often say they want their children to be happy, not realising they are conniving in keeping their children unhealthy through repression. Better to be real, to be conscious, to be sad when naturally sad, and happy when naturally happy.

29. Hate – *Hate is sustained and chosen anger in a given direction.* We usually hate others because of their shadow qualities, and we ourselves may be hated for the same reasons. To continually want someone out of your life, whether they are actually around or not, is to project your own shadow and hate it. For what can cause continual anger in oneself if not one's own shadow side, the part we try so hard to repress in ourselves? *All hate is self-hate, a secret loathing of a strong part of oneself. We are only ultimately angry at ourselves, and that is what we deal with.*

30. Healing – *Healing is bringing resolution to a situation, condition, confict or issue.* We all leave childhood feeling we need healing. Or if we do not feel it, then later in our lives we will fall sick with anxiety, physical illness or depression, and wonder what is wrong with us. *All illness is really the illness of having an unresolved childhood.* The original pain, and the shell we unconsciously and consciously built around it, has never been healed so that it reappears, especially under stress, in our adult lives. *To heal the adult heal the child in the adult.* All medical personnel know how much adult patients regress when forced to be in a hospital situation. There we must give up control, go back into a state of terror similar to childhood in which we experienced over and over again how we did not have control of our lives and what resulted from this. So as adults trying to control things we create stress, precipitating illness which cannot be cured until we let go and go with a healing process which brings resolution and new life, or if in extreme, death, which is both the relief of an unhappy life and childhood, and the final return, home at last.

31. Hurt – *Nobody can hurt us but ourselves.* Yes, we feel pain when some part of us is under attack, but to feel really hurt is to regress again into the wounded child, creating victims in adult life. Nobody is to blame. Nobody hurts another. Each person simply carries on life activity as best they can.

Sometimes this causes pain, suffering, the loss of something dear. But hurt, the identification with pain – I am not so sure. It takes some doing to get to the place where you can experience both pain and pleasure as equals in life, just different energy effects. To do this you must have come to terms with the pain of childhood, the trauma, and know this time what it is to be almost overwhelmed by the dark side, that which destroys. Then having found the victim in you, you no longer need to fall into a victimish space in which you constantly hurt. You have the choice of considering the pain you feel as a healing energy to be dealt with or as a hurt to be overwhelmed by, crying out in a thousand and one lamentations.

32. Inner Life – *Inner is prior to outer*. The inner life is what we were good at in childhood, beginning as babies experiencing the effects of energy and actions around us, as well as the internal states of our little bodies when we wanted to feed, shit, and so on. But then, when children, the adults, the culture, the school system, kept demanding that we come out of our interior worlds and become active in the exterior life. We learned to read other people's stories rather than keep creating those of our own. We learned to perform for tests and presentations. We learned to please the adults who were only interested, or so it seemed, in what we could do out there. So the inner life was almost neglected, the fantasies, the feelings, the natural values and insights from within, the intuitive grasp of reality. Instead we learned to substitute book learning, authoritative statements from others, and the whole ilk of what it is to be called civilised. Now as adults we feel a loss of energy and meaning in life. We have put too much of our vital energy outside ourselves. We know somewhere in our hearts that all the achievements, the rewards, the pay cheques, even the holidays are mostly for show, and therefore not real to us as beings because they are out there. Now we return to, and deal with, childhood to get back to the memories, the inner workings of the soul, of the psyche, what it is to be a child again capable of being alone with itself. We know that behind the adult life there is still the Myth of Childhood waiting to be born. As the accomplishments grow and fade away the memories do not go. They are the heralds, the flags that remain as signals of the way, whether lived ill or well, consciously or not, and still they are there, pointing backwards and forwards, the climax and circle of the inner life.

33. Joy – *Joy is the feeling experience of fulfilment*. We have worked hard. We have sacrificed. We have created. And now the actualisation of new potential is at hand. There is new life and this creates such a good feeling, that vital feeling when everything works together to create something real and valuable. There was so much joy in childhood, whether we remember it or not, in those moments when we lived well our spontaneous childness, creating with whatever was there in the moment. Now as adults we seek fulfilment, the accomplishment of what we have the potential for, what we are meant to do in life. We know this sense of fulfilment, not just in what we achieve, but in the joy which is part of and follows the creative act. If you do not feel joy and fulfilment after completing a project, then you have not fulfilled yourself, you have not brought enough of yourself to the work to be happy in it. Forget the externals. Winning at a game or in the work place or even in a relationship, means little if the natural joy is absent. To find what you are meant to do in life, commit yourself to doing only that which is possible and brings the natural joy of fulfilment. Stop working for others' expectations and start working for the deeper Self. You will know the difference between the false and the real in the joy you feel in accomplishment.

34. Laughter – It seems so natural to laugh, so why don't we do it more often? The children laugh and the adults are serious, unless they take something to relax them. Find a serious child and you find a child who has had to give up being a child early in order to assume an adult role in parenting a parent. In laughter we break the connection. If something goes wrong we break our identification with it so that we will not suffer too much. We laugh, and, hopefully, move on. Or when we do not want to stay with pain, we laugh or smile to break the spell. Some laughter, then, is avoidance. There is a time to break a connection to a person, thing, or event, and a time to keep the connection going until we get to our feelings and acknowledge them in action. Learn laughter from a child. They are closer to the absurdity of the world. What we take for granted they see as play. Through the child's eyes we can develop perspective.

35. Judgementalism – The difficulty with calling things good and bad is that we believe our categories. Murdering someone is not bad. It is murdering someone. It is destructive. Most of us severely dislike the act because of our strong instinct for self-preservation. In childhood too many of the parents and other authorities called what we did good or bad. They never said, 'I really like', or 'I really dislike, what you are doing'. They tried to fit us into categories of the absolute, as religions do. The result is judgementalism, the judging of another right or wrong, the calling of a person good or bad, wonderful or terrible. These statements extrovert the process. Calling someone else bad, rather than just saying, 'I feel bad when you do that', puts the responsibility out there for our own reactions. So we teach our children by calling them good or bad, and by calling their actions good or bad. To mature into adulthood is to accept all that happens as reality. To do this we can give up our categories. What you do not like, deal with, and what you love, deal with. Have your own reactions and leave the other person to deal with their own reactions. Do not judge them, even if you must oppose them for your own security.

36. Leaving Home – The important thing about leaving is that it replicates the primal leaving the womb and its attachments. We may have wanted to stay warm and protected, being taken care of. But there was also a pressure, as we grew larger, to be expelled from the womb. When the pressure is not there in the family to expel us out into the next stage of life, we may well create it by being rebellious, lazy, unco-operative. To break the connection, to cut the umbilical cord once again, is felt with pain. But we learn to do it, to move on in life. Yes, every gain has its loss, loss of womb, loss of connection. Better to experience it as it comes or we will resist change because we fear the suffering involved in breaking connections. So leaving home happens many times in our lives. Not just the original leave-taking, but in changing jobs and relationships, even in leaving each morning for work, or going on a holiday. Expect especially strong feelings at these transition times. Learn to prepare and go through the separation. There is always a gate to a new life, but only you can open it fully. You can be shoved up to the gate, but it is your choice whether you go through or not. Of course if you do not choose the next step, an abyss may fall away before you, plunging you *in extremis* into your future. Learn to leave home and there will be no turning back in life.

37. Life – *The miracle of life is that we exist to ourselves as well as to others*. Others are there to give us feedback that we exist. We enter a relationship, we find an object, a beloved, because it helps us define more who we are. Life, then, is not simply organic matter in movement, but existence itself. *To be known to oneself is life*. Not to be known is biological life but mental and spiritual death. In childhood we became awake to ourselves for the first time as an I, an ego. We recall our earliest dream and what it shows about the pattern we live and relive in our lives. *To exist we must define ourselves*. We must use the biological life to create consciousness of who we are and what life is all about. So the return to the childhood material is to get it more real this time round, to see the pattern of our destiny, our own unique way of doing things, and of dealing with the happenstance of fate, whether in the loss of a parent, a move elsewhere, or whatever big event which was outside our control. We want to have life consciously and not just unconsciously. We want, above all, to sense where life is going, where the greatest chance for fulfilment is. That is a mighty task. To come alive to life takes all our doing.

38. Love – The problem of love in adult life is that most of us feel we did not receive enough love as children. True! The need for love is often greater than the capacity to love. *Greater than love is the need for love*. In childhood we could hardly learn to love the child in us if the others did not love the child which we were. In adult life we seek and seek for someone to at last love the child within, and often we are disappointed. But not always. There are loving people in this life, people who have realised that the way to receive love is to love wholeheartedly, without domination by ulterior motives. You will manipulate for love if you cannot yourself love freely without thought of external reward. *The problem of love is to find the needy child in us and fulfil it*. Then we will be able to love others as well as ourselves. *Love is the ability to care for and affirm the potential for new life.* Each stroke, each caress, which makes us feel good is also an evocation, a signal, that we are awake and alive to ourselves and to another. *To love another do only those things which are loving of yourself as well.* If you are in any way loving another to get love yourself you will do things like give sex, affection, and nurturing to get love, the affirmation of your own being. It will not work well, for the other person will sense neediness and will not want to respond, even if response is possible. *Learn to love the child in you and you will love the adult as well.*

39. Money Problems – *Money problems come down to a lack of positive self image and a weak reality function.* If we did not learn in childhood the fundamental lesson that there is a price for everything, then as adults we will not have the right attitudes for valuing the results of our labour in just payment for our work. We will spend, or not spend, unrealistically. We will not seek good work which is personally and financially fulfilling. It matters if you do not bring up your children to pay the price for being cared for. If they do not have chores, or if you do not insist they do them, you are teaching them not to see consequences for their actions, and it will go worse for them in the real world of adult life. *Teach reality in the home and the children will learn reality in the adult life.*

40. Mother – *Every act of bonding is a reattachment to the mother for new life and nurturing.* So in making love with a partner of either sex we are reattaching to the Great Mother for renewal and life. The mother as the font of nurturing is everywhere in life, not just in sexual or eating experience. We learn to seek it out and make it conscious, rather than burden any one person or activity for all our mothering needs. We all need reconnection to the sources of life. Those who are successfully nurtured on an ongoing basis are less dependent than those who inhibit themselves, waiting and hoping for affirmation and nurturing, being too afraid to go out and get restoration where it is available. We learn not to idealise life but to reconnect to life for constant renewal. Those who try to conserve what they have, inevitably dry up. Those who express and expend what they are given, and also seek replenishment at the source, will find new life over and over again as they journey down the path of their own chosen destiny.

41. Nightmares – In the night dreams come to present us with the issues of our lives. In childhood we may have had dreams which spoke directly to our fear of being overwhelmed. Feeling overwhelmed to the child is best described as loss of self, of personal identity. The child is made to do things which are not felt as a natural expression of itself at that stage in life, like having to be sexual before being emotionally or physically ready. It's not the offence itself which is detrimental, it is the loss of personal identity, of who the person is and is becoming. Thus nightmares feature our dream ego as about to be overwhelmed, be it from a big wave or a killing hand. Lack of self existence is destructive because it limits our ability to know who we are or to make choices which affirm who we feel we are. We have weak choice making and ability to cope with reality as it is. The nightmare comes and shocks us into awareness of how ill equipped we are to deal with things. Perhaps the shock is good if it serves as a motivation to the child and to the adult to become more self aware and affirming. *Nightmares are issued needing resolution.* If we exist at all we can keep affirming ourselves and becoming stronger in what we will deal with in life. For one of the great tasks of life is to deal with all of life, more and more as it comes, without closing off to any part. This is what it means to go *where the fear is, and to live at the edge of risk.*

42. Parenting – How can we expect parents who have never been well parented to parent their own children well? We cannot. They may do a better job than their parents, but even here they may go to an extreme by giving their children all the nurturing they never had. *You cannot redeem your own childhood by being a good parent to your children. You only redeem childhood by working on the inner child, and by bringing your inner parent to it.* The best healing in having kids is what these outer children bring up of your own childhood and how you deal with it. Too much focus on outer children, even your own, takes you away from yourself and becomes a burden to them as well. For what children need is to develop themselves, following their own inner sources, not the expectations of the adults which are based on projecting their own inner children out onto their outer children. *You best parent others by parenting yourself.* Whatever you do for your child, learn to do for yourself as well. Use your children as catalysts for your own growth, and you might just achieve enough objectivity to stay out of their hair most of the time. The best parent is one who parents him or herself.

43. Perspective – *Perspective is the context through which you see life.* If you do not have a conscious context you will have an unconscious patterning through which you react to life. Better to become active in life than reactive to life. We use The Myth of Childhood here as one of our perspectives about life. Our key point is that we repeat over and over again in adult life the unresolved dynamics and patterns originally created in childhood, and that we cannot become mature adults until we have resurrected and dealt with the childhood material. We go even further to suggest that many perspectives on life, like that of most religions, are really a symbolic replication of the childhood experience, such as seeking in the God image the parenting we never had. So our method is to first make conscious our perspective on life, and then to choose the perspective, principles and practices by which we will live. This way we need not be dominated by the childhood experience and can therefore fulfil ourselves.

44. Power – The key issue in power is whether to use it or not. Each of us is given far more energy than we utilise in life. In childhood we begin repressing our natural energy because the adults are suppressing it in us. They do not like small children running about constantly and getting into things. They do not like having to be with the child all the time to give him and her creative things to do. And so suppression leads to repression. The child learns to hold back and keep down or it will be hurt. Most of us do not enter adult life raring to go and in full command of the energy available to us. *Power is the ability to use energy effectively.* In order to get something done you must have the energy and the means to do it. You must earn money and learn how to lead other people so that you may use their energy as well. We learn to play the power game. Where we go wrong is in trying to amass power for power's sake, as in going for more and more money or political power. *Better to seek values and potentials which add to the meaning of life and use the maximum power available to actualise those values and potentials.* If you have retreated into idealising by rejecting reality, originally your childhood, as it is, then you will not seek power to realise your values. The idealists eschew power, preferring instead to remain aloof and critical of the world. The realists can, for their part, seek power for power's sake and lose sight of what it means to use power to actualise values. The integrated person does not hesistate to go for maximum power and value in a world which is real. To graduate from childhood is to accept the world as it is, and to better it.

45. Projection – *We project what we have not yet made conscious.* Looking back to childhood we can see how we were in a constant state of projection. We thought our parents were wonderful. We saw terrors in the dark. Gradually as we grew up we learned to take more and more of what we put out there back inside. Through integration we became more of a person. And this is the process, to first project inner material, and then to make it conscious and integrate it within ourselves. We turn image into function. First the parents are outside in action and image, and then they can be seen as inside as we carry out the parental function ourselves, both with others and with ourself. When we think we are talking about someone else we are really talking about ourselves. Parents tell us stories about their children, but what they say is what they have projected onto the child. For we all have selective memory. If we are feeling bad we will see bad in the world. We learn also that people project onto us, they see us in a different light from how we see ourselves. A major move out of childhood is to no longer identify with people's projections onto us. Do they love us? That is a projection of their own part needing love. Do they rage against us to others? That is the part within themselves, which they cannot stand, that they are talking about. We learn then in the midst of all the projections coming our way to counterbalance them with the exercise of self-definition. You say I am like that. This is how I see myself. *What we see in others is really in ourselves. What others see in us is what they need to see in themselves.*

46. Reality – The key to the whole process is facing reality, a difficult feat for most people. To test yourself ask, do you accept all of life as it is and deal with it effectively? Or do you reject certain aspects of life, calling them bad, and avoid and flee from them? Do you use fantasy to escape from your everyday life, or do you use fantasy to discover new potential in yourself and in life to actualise? In childhood we learned to escape into fantasy and to seek only the positive. We gained a distorted view of the way the world is, especially if our parents were overprotective. Now as adults there is nowhere to go. We can escape into imagination, dreams, sleep, drugs, alcohol, meditation, children, work, and other forms of unconsciousness, but for how long? Eventually the suffering, based on what we have not dealt with, becomes too intense and we must seek help and healing. Reality is the real cure. Accept life as it is. Make your compromise with what is. Choose to want to be here because this is the only arena for fulfilment you have. Welcome home! If you can accept your childhood for what it was by working it through, then you can accept all of adult life and deal with it. You have that choice, at least for now!

47. Rejection – Nobody can reject us but ourselves. They can say No to us, but because someone says No to us, do we have to say No to ourselves? The rejection problem is a key because fear of rejection inhibits many people from fulfilling themselves. If you look to a small child you will see someone active in her own process. When she wants something she goes for it and sometimes receives a No and sometimes a Yes. *If you can take No for an answer you can ask for anything*. If you can take Yes for an answer you will have life. Yes, we were rejected in childhood, we were denied, neglected, made fun of, criticised, and left to our own devices. But so what? What is wrong with deprivation, unless because of it we close off to seeking the fullness of life? *If someone says No to you, say Yes to yourself*. Do not greet someone's No with an automatic exercise in self-criticism – what did I do wrong? Instead, affirm yourself. Recognise, if true, that what you wanted was good for both of you, and in saying No some people deny themselves the fullness of life. This is not your responsibility. You offered to share life. They rejected the opportunity for themselves. Hopefully they will find what they need elsewhere. That is their loss more than yours. For you are not stopped by others rejecting themselves. You move on to the next opportunity, secure in the knowledge that you will meet those like yourself, also saying Yes to life.

48. Relationship – We relate to others to relate to ourselves. We are born into relationship. We are not whole or entire unto ourselves. We need others and others need us. Better to recognise the simple fact of interdependence than get caught in codependence. Codependence is when we seek to use each other for our own needs. Interdependence is when we companion and give to each other what we ourselves have freely. I relate to you to express myself. I find in you the receiver and giver of life energy. You

234

are capable of doing both, and so I can do likewise. In relationship, we balance the energy. What we give out we also take in. What we receive we give again. Yet in childhood we learned a different relating. We learned that the adults wanted much from us and gave little. Or with some adults they gave much but did not receive well what we had to give. The relationship was unequal between parent and child because the parent either gave too much or too little. We learned that relationships were unbalanced and we could do little about it. But now in adult life why put up any longer with an imbalanced relationship?

49. Sadness – There is an infinite well of tears underlying life, and that is as it should be. Each day we walk in our own mortality, meeting fate and destiny. Each day we fail and succeed in life. Our sadness is the natural losses which occur, the unlived life that must drain into the past, the creative starts which are never to go anywhere, the accomplishments, however great, which must be given up now as we move on. This moment cannot last and that is the saddest of all. For we have known riches as well as deprivation, and we realise as well that some day we will know and live no more. An unhappy face is a great face as much as a smiling face is. The weight of childhood is sometimes heavy, and God help us if we were told to be happy all the time as children. Better to suffer well than to repress. For in suffering we free ourselves for joy, in sadness we cleanse ourselves of regret so that we can laugh again, cherishing the moment as it comes. To recapture again what it is like to be truly sad, remember childhood, the loneliness, the losses, the failed plans, the gifts never received, the endless quarrels, the countless difficulties. These, too, are real and part of the quality of life. Then as adults we can have our moments and share them with those who can accept and understand. We do not have to be happy all the time any longer. The burden of a too onesided life has been lifted from our shoulders as we allow ourselves to participate in the communal grief of the ages.

50. Sex – Ah sex! The danger is that we substitute this greatest of experiences for fulfilment. What did we do before sex in childhood? How did we fulfil ourselves? Well, we sought plenty of hugs. We tried to be close and touch as much as we could. We expressed joy and sadness in our play. We were feeling as children, and maybe we have lost much of that in adult life? In sex we can return to childhood again, to feel the primal mother in contact with our partner, the intense energy, the play, the laughter, the feelings, the creativity involved. Sex seems like fulfilment since it has a terrific energy buildup and release. But the same is true for actualising potential. Find what will fulfil you, where the centre in you wants to go, and then do what is necessary to actualise your potential.

51. Sickness – The key to sickness is whether we are in balance or not. Extreme stress equals sickness. If we are extreme in anything, from sex to sports to work to laziness, we will unbalance our energy system. Sickness is the opposite to intense vitality. Too much vitality expressed will cause regression. All the wounds of childhood are your sickness. If you did not learn it then, learn now to balance your energy. You alone are responsible. To go to a medical person because you are imbalanced may be necessary, but hardly a cure. The only cure is to learn to balance your life energy in all that you do. For this we need to know how we feel in each moment and how to transform compulsions into choice. Sickness regresses us to childhood moods and dynamics so that we may deal with imbalance there at new levels. Balance as a child balances by including and expressing the opposites. Then sickness will be embraced by you as one of the aspects of health.

52. Spiritual Perspective – In childhood we may have had experiences of something much larger than ourselves which gave us awe and the secret knowledge that a great mystery lay before us which it might take the rest of our lives to know. Before sexuality and our focus in the world were the young transcendent years, the years of innate knowing, of being a part of things greater while not yet fully immersed in the world. Then the world took over and we tried to change our focus from inner to outer in order to fit in and survive. Now again as adults we understand that material and outer reality is not enough. The mystery still lies there hidden behind things. What are the principles by which I choose to live my life? What gives life its meaning? For what purpose am I born? How can I fulfil the purpose of life for myself and for others? The spiritual perspective is both a disidentification from the world and a seeking for the core reality which underlies the world, the principles, the source energies, the purpose and destiny for which each of us is born. We want to find that and live it now while we still have the fullness of life. Death awaits us. Before that is the door, the gateway to mystery.

53. Suffering – The issue around suffering is to learn how to experience it creatively, without identifying with it. The issue of childhood is the issue of suffering. Some had it too hard with violence and neglect. Some had it too soft with overprotection and too much giving. Either extreme does not teach us how to go through the fire to spiritual and psychological transformation. In re-experiencing the childhood material the wound arises. Perhaps we all start with a poor relationship to pain, to hurt, to suffering. We condemn it as undesirable. We flee from it into experiences of pleasure. We repress it as too intense to be dealt with. We cause it through our compulsive acts. We are again called to look at and experience our suffering, the natural wound that we are heir to, but this time with acceptance and a commitment to deal with the dynamic no matter what. *Only the ego experiences suffering, and all suffering seems to be because we are attached to or identified with something which needs to go in the face of reality.* Were we completely with whatever is happening, and able to make the necessary shifts in the moment to encompass it, we would hardly suffer at all. So much agony is due to holding on, to wanting things to be a certain way. Look at why and when you are in pain and ask, what is being required of me to let go of? Then sacrifice and become free. *To resist life causes pain. To go with life gives the freedom to create with whatever is happening, and therein is fulfilment and meaning.*

54. Tears – Instead of crying call it releasing. When the tears come we are letting go to loss, to pain, to releasing feelings which have been pent up. And some tears are full of anger as well. Perhaps we felt so frustrated as a child we could not express ourselves and then dissolved into tears. In adult life we may do the same thing by weakening and letting go when we might better hold to our purpose. There is a time to release and a time to stay firm, and blessed is she or he who knows the difference. Sometimes stop your tears so that you may feel anger, or may firm up your resolve rather than weakening yourself by identifying with your vulnerability. Other times the release is what heals, the letting go of control and expressing vulnerability. Know your own tears as you choose to shed or not shed them. Be aware of what issues and themes move you and why. Know your childhood release pattern, the tears, the anger, or was it simply years of repression so that you showed no emotion which could get you into trouble?

55. Unfairness – Whoever said the world was fair? Did God say this? Or is fairness something you ardently desire in life? To the child fairness is 'I get what other children are getting'. That is fair. But reality dictates otherwise Sometimes there will be enough of life's energy for everybody. Other times someone will make a choice to meet their own needs first and consequently neglect you. Nothing wrong with that. Adjust! What you cannot find in one place you may find elsewhere. If you spend even an ounce of energy protesting about what you did not get, you will waste energy and make it harder then to get what you need. When one door closes, open another. Do not stay at the old door and bang away forever. The door is closed, my friend. Go elsewhere. Yes, we seek to balance energy in life, but that does not mean we always have experiences of balance. When in imbalance we try to rebalance, or let our position go so that a new balance may come about. *If things are not going your way, change your way so that you may be where things are going well.*

Appendix 2
Definitions

Abuse: A destructive act done towards someone weaker than the perpetrator which traumatises the victim, making it difficult or impossible to live a fulfilling life.

Acceptance: The choice to open oneself to the way things are.

Actualising Dreams: The practice of re-experiencing dreams and the bringing of their content into everyday life.

Anger: The emotion of repressed feeling. When we do not express but repress we are causing life energy to dam up until it explodes into anger.

Archetype: A cluster of energy and form inherent in existence. A basic pattern of energy expression which manifests as energy and form, as image, as pattern, as functions within the personality and outside in society, as feelings, and finally as concepts and symbols.

Choice: The directing of energy in one direction and not another. The saying Yes to one thing while saying No to all that would oppose it.

Consciousness: Awareness plus appropriate action. To be truly aware is to act on that awareness.

Destiny: What we do with fate through choice. We do not choose what happens to us but we can choose how we deal with what happens.

Dialogue: A dreamwork and journalwork method in which you access dynamics in your psyche other than ego and give them a voice.

Dream Ego: The focus of the dreamer's self-identity while in the dream. This may be the dreamer's image or merely a felt presence of awareness without specific form, or even awareness but in another form.

Dream Re-entry: A dreamwork method in which you place yourself in a meditative state and go back into your dream from the waking state in order to re-experience your dream more fully and possibly resolve it.

Dream Source: That centre within the psyche which uses the image-making function of the psyche to create inner experiences of meaning when the person is asleep.

Dream: An inner experience in action, feeling, imagery, and sometimes word which is produced by non-ego sources, namely the Dream Source.

Dreamwork: Working with dreams to enhance their content and bring out the meaning they have for the dreamer.

Ego: The personality function which focuses awareness, makes choices, and is the locus of individual identity.

Emotion: An over-riding energy state in the psyche which subverts specific feeling states to its mood.

Feeling: The experience of either positive (going towards) or negative (withdrawing) energy within, which then gets expressed in voice or action.

Feminine: The archetype of openness, flow, and encompassing reality.

God: Non-ego source energy of greater power and wisdom than the ego can, of itself, create. Other terms: Source, Divinity, Sacred, Dream, Reality.

Individuation: A life-long process of becoming conscious about one's own true nature and following that nature rather than collective values and attitudes. Ongoing dreamwork is necessary to discovering and following one's own inner nature.

Inner Experience: Mental and physical states felt and perceived as coming from within and expressed in feeling, imagery, action and concept.

Intuition: The direct perception of the potential and inherent character of a thing or experience.

Journey: The experience of integrating one's inner awareness and development with one's outer awareness and development. Also, a sense of living one's inherent predisposition and purpose in life.

Mandala Dreamwork Training: A complete dreamwork approach combining a full dreamwork methodology with a strong perspective on the nature of the human spiritual and psychological journey.

Life Force: The energy, the ability to move matter, within oneself and one's life.

Masculine: The archetype of focus, direction, and goal orientation.

Meditative State: A mental state of inner awareness in which the ego allows inner dynamics to unfold.

Myth of Childhood: The core pattern in us which still governs and influences our adult behaviour until we have made it conscious and transformed it.

Numinous: The energy-giving or creative aspect of a symbol or sacred experience.

Objectivity: Perceiving the inherent nature of a thing based on perceiving both our own subjective bias and experiencing directly the object of our awareness out there.

Observing Ego: The individual point of awareness which observes actions and other mental states and has self-identity.

Opposites: Primary energies or archetypes which exist in relation to each other through harmony and opposition.

Pain: The experience of resisting the life force.

Participating Ego: The individual point of awareness with self-identity which also involves itself in an experience and takes action.

Persona: The positive side of the personality made up of self-identity images and attitudes which are considered positive by the individual and possibly the culture within which he or she dwells.

Pleasure: The experience of the life force flowing freely through one.

To Process: To reveal hidden dynamics and issues by making them conscious and experiencing their effects at a feeling level. Then making choices to resolve the issues or integrate the dynamics involved.

Psyche: The totality of the inner world of a person which has the integrative centre of the Self, the dynamics of the unconscious, the ego, the persona, the shadow, and other dynamics such as the parent-child complexes and archetypal manifestations.

Reality: That which is by force of its being. The effect of energy and matter which over-rides the subjective symbol-systems of the individual.

Religion: A collective belief and practice occurring in groups of people.

Resistance: The attempt by the ego and other parts of the psyche to remain within known patterns and attitudes in the face of new growth.

Resolution: The Art of initiating a change in a pattern or situation of conflict, which then allows any of its dynamics to be harmonised or destroyed.

Self: Capitalised, the Self is the integrative centre within the personality. It utilises the archetype of centre in the universe itself, and so may also refer to the centre which is in all things.

Sex: The experiencing of the life force through the central archetype of unity.

Shadow: That side of the personality which is hidden from the persona – the conscious side – due to the ego's identification with the persona.

240

Soul: A word for referring to the relationship between the ego and the centre of the psyche and of life. The soul is the personal aspect of the Self.

Spiritual: The experience of source energies other than ego which happen to the individual. Spiritual experience occurs only to individuals and is direct and not based on collective belief and practice.

Subjective: The inner mental processes which colour our perceptions of what is outside us.

Suffering: The tension between a person's present and emotional state and the new state demanded by forces greater than ego.

Symbol Immersion: A meditative state technique for experiencing images and actions at an inner level.

Symbol System: A loosely organised conglomeration of images, attitudes and concepts which the individual and societies use as the basis for organising their behaviour and making choices. No symbol system is reality itself but only an approximation of what the perceivers assert reality is like.

Symbol: A cluster of images and energy which evokes many levels of meaning.

Synchronicity: Meaningful coincidence. The convergence of separately happening events and dynamics, inner and outer, which together produce a meaningful pattern involving the specific consciousness of a person.

Truth: That which is real by direct knowing, either through experience or through intuition, the direct perceiving of core essences behind manifestations of the concrete.

Unconscious: A term used for that part of the psyche which we can never know consciously. The Unconscious is only one part of the total psyche.

Wholeness: An on-going process of making conscious and including all parts of oneself, including the shadow side, within a harmonising and differentiating whole.

Contact Addresses

For those interested in working further with this approach please contact the following authorised centres for Mandala Dreamwork Training. Our training programmes generally require a year or more commitment, and are for professionals and serious lay people on a journey.

Journey Centre – Scotland
Hilary Scaife, Director
2 Quarryford Farm Cottages, Haddington
East Lothian EH41 4PL SCOTLAND

Bauker Kurisgård Senter
2621 Østre Gausdal
NORWAY

For writing to the author or obtaining information about his books and tapes, please contact the publishers or:

Journey Press – Publisher's Services
PO Box 2510
Novato, CA94948
USA

Further Reading

Changing Your Life Strephon Kaplan-Williams, Journey Press, 1987.
Also published as *The Practice of Personal Transformation* The
Aquarian Press, 1986.
This book is a chief reference work since it has detailed methods
and background on working with the dynamics of the psyche, such
as choice-making, attitude change, anger, love, and so on.

Jungian Senoi Dreamwork Manual Strephon Kaplan-Williams, Journey
Press, 1980. Also published as, *The Dreamwork Manual* The
Aquarian Press, 1984.
This work offers a complete and practical dreamwork approach
necessary for those readers who choose to follow their dreams at
the same time they are working on their childhood material.

The Elements of Dreamwork, Strephon Kaplan-Williams, Element Books,
1990.
A short book on the basics of dreamwork and its application to life,
relationships and healing.

The Inner World of Childhood Francis Wickes, Sigo Press, 1988.
This book is a real classic. It contains excellent material which is
highly recommended.

The Drama of the Gifted Child Alice Miller, Basic Books, Inc./Harper
Colophon Books. Also published as, *The Drama of Being a Child*
Virago Press, 1987.
This also is a classic whose main thesis seems to be that much is
done by adults to limit the natural growth of the child.

The Origins and History of Consciousness Eric Neumann, Routledge &
Kegan Paul.
This is the great Jungian work on the emergence of consciousness
out of childhood into adult years.

The New Diary Tristine Rainer, Jeremy Tarcher, and Angus &
Robertson, 1980.
The best book, despite its title, specifically on journal writing,
written with a sense of creativity and ease.

Index